How to Get Yourself to Do What You Want to Do

How to Get Yourself to Do What You Want to Do

Paul E. Wood, M.D.

PRENTICE-HALL, INC., Englewood Cliffs, New Jersey

*How to Get Yourself to Do What You
Want to Do* by Paul E. Wood, M.D.

Copyright © 1981 by Paul E. Wood, M.D.
All rights reserved. No part of this book may be
reproduced in any form or by any means, except
for the inclusion of brief quotations in a review,
without permission in writing from the publisher.
Address inquiries to Prentice-Hall, Inc., Englewood
Cliffs, N.J. 07632.
Printed in the United States of America
Prentice-Hall International, Inc., London
Prentice-Hall of Australia, Pty. Ltd., Sydney
Prentice-Hall of Canada, Ltd., Toronto
Prentice-Hall of India Private Ltd., New Delhi
Prentice-Hall of Japan, Inc., Tokyo
Prentice-Hall of Southeast Asia Pte. Ltd., Singapore
Whitehall Books Limited, Wellington, New Zealand

10 9 8 7 6 5 4 3 2 1

Library of Congress Cataloging in Publication Data

Wood, Paul, Date
  How to get yourself to do what you want to do.

  Includes index.
  1. Success. I. Title.
BF637.S8W67   158.1   80-25711
ISBN 0-13-409854-4

To all my patients who taught me the lessons in this book; and to Don who taught me the lessons of Loving, Honoring, Trusting, and Playing.

Contents

Introduction

Most people go through life complaining about all of the things they think are wrong with themselves. They nag at themselves, feel guilty, put themselves down, and in general keep themselves feeling at least somewhat negative about themselves most of the time. Rarely do any of us come face to face with ourselves, reviewing what we feel must be changed and then taking the necessary steps to make that change. This book discloses the defenses and methods we use to keep ourselves from changing and offers simple, concrete, and effective techniques for making significant changes in our lives.

This approach to changing yourself was developed out of my experience treating several thousand persons in my psychiatric practice. It is not a theoretical approach based on great and small psychological truths. It is based on real people solving real problems, and in many cases making dramatic changes in their lives. The accomplishment of significant changes is not an easy task. It takes hard work, decision, and commitment. However, the process is not complicated or confusing, and it doesn't need to take a long time. You can begin changing yourself immediately using these simple, straightforward techniques. On the other hand, if you think you want to change something about yourself but you are not really sure, this method will quickly clarify your motivation to change and enable you to make a conscious choice to either change or stay the way you are, without guilt. You will be able to say, "I know I could change myself but I am choosing not to."

Finally, a word about the development of this approach. Like so many other inventions, this approach to helping people change themselves came out of frustration and need. Confronted daily with patients who had been in therapy for years with minimal change, I knew there had to be a better way. Experience working with children and their families led to the development of Brief Family Intervention, which is a rapidly effective technique of helping parents change their children's behavior. This work, published under the title, "How to Get Your Children to Do What You Want Them to Do," received wide acceptance and acclaim. (Paul Wood and Bernard Schwartz, Prentice-Hall, Englewood Cliffs, N.J., 1977.) The techniques of changing children's behavior apply equally well to the adult wishing to change his or her own behavior. Of course several modifications are required, but the basic techniques are the same, and the results are comparable.

Paul E. Wood, M.D.

Chapter 1

What's Your Problem?

What do you want to change about yourself?

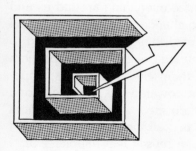

At various times in our lives we all go through periods in which we think we should change something about ourselves. It might be overweight, smoking, drinking, our relationships with others, or our own internal rotten feelings. The list of possibilities for personal change is endless, but for each of us there are a limited number of alternatives from which we must choose. The first step is to sort out the really significant issues from everything else in our lives.

Most of us work very hard at avoiding making changes in our lives; we do this by keeping ourselves confused. We practice fuzzy thinking, which keeps us in a perplexed, limbo state. We know that we are not happy with ourselves and our lives but we feel we just don't know what to do to change things. We complain and criticize everything around us and believe that the world needs to change in order for us to feel better. People who practice fuzzy thinking avoid coming to grips with specifically what they are doing which keeps them feeling so bad. They think of themselves as helpless, hopeless, overwhelmed, and overpowered by the big world around them. These people often speak in vague generalities about their plight: "I just feel bad all the time," or "I wish I knew what I could do to make myself feel happier," or "I don't think there is anything that can help me." They unconsciously convince themselves that they are doomed to be stuck in their personal hell by their thoughts and behaviors. The great advantage of fuzzy thinking is that it keeps us from ever having to do anything differently. As long as we stay confused and unclear, there is no obvious problem and therefore no place to begin to make change, and therefore nobody, including ourselves, can expect us to do so.

The first step in getting yourself to do what you want to

do is to decide exactly and specifically what you want to do differently. An example may help to clarify.

Mrs. Lee is a 42-year-old 300-pound, five foot, four inch woman. She is obviously grossly overweight. On her first appointment I asked her what her problem was and she replied, "I just don't know what's wrong with me. I'm unhappy all the time. I have no energy, I can't get along with anyone, and I just don't know what to do with myself."

I questioned, "What is the most important thing you want to change first about yourself?" She replied, "Well, maybe I should go on a diet." I asked, "To gain, maintain, or lose weight?" Mrs. Lee responded somewhat indignantly, "Why to lose, of course." I clarified, "Going on a diet has nothing to do with losing weight. I am sure you have been on hundreds of diets during your life and have probably lost hundreds of pounds but here you are today at 300 pounds. It is clear that you are practicing unclear, fuzzy thinking about your weight and diets. You have never clarified that you are going to lose X number of pounds and maintain that loss for the rest of your life." Mrs. Lee replied, "Well I guess when you put it that way, I never have because I'm not sure I can do it." I supported, "As long as you have any doubts or questions about your capabilities of being successful, you will continue to let yourself off the hook by using fuzzy thinking and unclear communications to yourself which make no demands for change."

Thinking about ourselves in terms of exact and specific behaviors gives us a clear picture of what needs to be changed. There are really only two possibilites for change. We want to either start doing something differently, or stop some particular behavior. It is that simple. For instance, you might want to start meeting new people to develop some new friends (combating aloneness and loneliness); you might wish to enroll in some classes to explore your interests and potentials (career choice or change); you might want to read a book or take a course in assertion skills and practice what you learned (overcoming shyness and inhibitions with people). On the other hand, you might want to stop drinking or smoking, stop associating with people you don't like, or stop eating too much. In each case, the behavior to be accomplished is clear and precise. How you will go about achieving the desired behavior becomes much easier once you have clarified exactly and specifically what you want do. As in the case of Mrs. Lee, until she narrowed her problems down to losing weight, she felt overwhelmed and confused about herself and did nothing. Once she decided that losing weight and maintaining the loss was the first thing she was going to do, she was well on her way to success and no longer felt the helpless, hopeless feelings of confusion and despair.

Some of you may be thinking, "But my problem is not any particular kind of behavior, it is how I feel." This is another example of confused thinking. As long as you keep your problems at a feeling level you will only be able to agonize over them. For every feeling there are behaviors that coincide. Trying to change the feelings first almost never works, because the behaviors that support those feelings persist. If you change the behaviors, the changed feelings will follow. Many of the traditional counseling and psychotherapeutic approaches focus on understanding and changing feelings in the hope that the behaviors will change. The large number of persons who persist in their subtle and overt self-destructive behaviors while steeped in therapy attest to the inefficiency of this method.

Examine the feelings that you have and then look at the behaviors you are engaging in which reinforce that feeling. Remember for every feeling there must be associated behaviors which support the belief that you feel that way. For example, if you feel shy and afraid of people you will be avoiding people by staying in your house much of the time. You will avoid exposing yourself to crowds of people in shopping centers, church meetings, etc. because you know it would make you feel nervous. By such behavior you prove to yourself over and over that you are not able to be among people without feeling upset.

Mr. DeFranco, a middle-aged, unmarried man, is an engineer in a large aerospace company. He lives alone in a small one-bedroom apartment where most of his neighbors are retired persons. He has no close friends and after working hard each day comes home to his lonely apartment, fixes himself a TV dinner, and watches television until he goes to bed. His weekends and holidays are spent in essentially the same manner. Upon coming to therapy, he described himself as very lonely and depressed and he questioned why he should go on living. He stated clearly at the outset that he did not think psychotherapy could help him but he would come one time to please his only sister, who lived two thousand miles away and who was worried about him. During the initial interview, Mr. DeFranco revealed that he had always been a "loner" and had always felt that life didn't have much to offer him. As a child he had had one or two close friends and in college, although he isolated himself, he was involved in the engineering club and was especially interested in electronic toys and gadgets. He had not pursued his electronics interest since college. Mr. DeFranco had not been on a date or attended any social event since college and felt that no woman would be interested in him. He viewed himself as unattractive and undesirable. A review of his current activities revealed that he was meeting his expectations and beliefs about himself one hundred percent. He was constantly isolating himself at work and at home and reinforcing his negative view of himself as a loner and undesirable person. He was not behaving in any ways which would make him feel better about himself.

The first step in the treatment process was to ascertain what he wanted to do differently. He said he wanted to feel better and enjoy life more. Questioning about what would make him feel better and what he would enjoy revealed that he wanted some friends and wanted to get out of his apartment more. He agreed to do whatever he had to do to help himself, if he could be certain that he would feel better. I prescribed that he speak to five new people in the following week and that he check out the possibilities of some kind of electronics club or group at his work and in the community. The following week Mr. DeFranco reported that he had spoken to seven people at work and in a shopping center near his apartment where he spent Saturday afternoon. He also had discovered at his company an electronics club of engineers who worked primarily on developing electronic toys and gadgets for fun. He had met the president of the club and planned on attending their next meeting. He related that he really felt uncomfortable talking to all these strangers but at the same time he felt a certain sense of relief at having spoken to other people. The next week's assignment was to get to know one person a little better and to plan on having lunch eventually with that person. In addition, he was to begin an exercise program of daily twenty-minute jogging to increase his feelings of self-worth and get himself out of the house. In the following four weeks Mr. DeFranco joined the electronics club and spent three evenings a week working on a special project with two other engineers. He also had lunch with a middle-aged widow who worked as receptionist for the company and he was planning on seeing more of her. All of these new behaviors were very hard for Mr. DeFranco, but he recognized that if he didn't change his behavior he was never going to feel any better. He terminated therapy after the sixth session, saying he was feeling so much better about himself and his life and that he no longer felt the need for the therapeutic contact. Approximately one year later I received an announcement of the marriage of Mr. DeFranco and the receptionist he had been dating.

This case underscores the concept that people who behave in positive successful ways tend to feel good about themselves. It is unusual for people who are behaving in a successful manner to feel depressed about themselves for very long periods of time. That is not to say that even the most positive and successful behaving people don't get the "blues" now and then, but these episodes tend to be short-lived and essentially insignificant. It is also important to note that the changes which Mr. DeFranco undertook had nothing to do with any exploration of *why* he was feeling the way he was. No time was spent looking at his childhood experiences or trying to find any excuses for his current behavior. The therapy was concerned only with the negative, self-destructive behaviors and provided counteracting positive, self-productive behaviors to replace them. No deep psychological insight was required. In fact, if we had focused on insight into why Mr. DeFranco felt the way he did, there is little likelihood that any significant change would have occurred merely because Mr. DeFranco had learned why he believed himself to be incapable of making friends and enjoying life more. The insight often serves as an excuse for the negative behavior and the excuses tend to perpetuate the behavior. Focusing on feelings usually only results in understanding and reinforcing those feelings. Furthermore, a commonly overlooked fault of understanding or insight is that in order to understand why you are behaving the way you are, you must continue to behave in that manner in order to pursue the understanding. Most people are not interested in discussing why they used to have certain behaviors, but rather are concerned about their current behaviors. If the behavior in question is stopped, then there is nothing to gain insight or understanding about. It is only when we maintain the behavior that we are willing to invest our time and money in talking about it. In short, you will always get faster and better results focusing on changing behaviors rather than attempting to understand them.

You may think that this simple-sounding method doesn't apply to you because your problem has been present for a long time. There is no evidence to suggest that long-standing behavior patterns are much more difficult to change than recently developed ones. In both cases, the patterns of behavior have become a customary way of being. Cigarette smoking, before-dinner cocktails, the large evening meal, dessert after dinner, and almost all other behaviors which we repeat and anticipate are merely habit patterns. They may have started out as something we wanted to do but after a few repetitions they became habitual. Habits are merely learned ways of behaving. They are not instincts or in any way predetermined or preconditioned. We try something and if we like it, we repeat it. With enough repetitions the behavior takes on a pattern which becomes part of who we think we are and we work very hard to protect the pattern as part of ourself. It is for this reason that so many people tenaciously hang on to their habit patterns even when all the evidence suggests they should give them up; frequently such old habit patterns are not even enjoyable any more. They literally become a part of our identity: I am a cigarette smoker; or I always *have* to have dessert in order to feel complete after a meal. In some cases habits become so ingrained that the person is not even consciously aware of the behavior, for instance, the smoker who lights a new cigarette while another is burning in the ashtray, or the person who eats exactly the same breakfast at the same time every day of the year, or the person who *must* have a drink in order to feel comfortable in a crowd of new people. None of these behaviors is necessary for a person's well-being, yet there is a very strong resistance to change.

Since habits are just learned ways of behaving, they can of course, be changed or unlearned. All that is required is the decision to change and then continual conscious awareness to make the change and not fall back into the unconscious habit pattern. Because our habits are repeated so frequently they are at least partly out of our conscious minds. For instance, if you drive the same way to work each day you are doing it primarily out of habit and using very little of your conscious mind. This is why you can formulate your plans for the day, rehearse speeches, or make out a shopping list while driving your usual route. If you change the route in any way you will have to use your conscious mind to get you there; otherwise, you need pay very little attention to the driving, as your habit-patterned behavior will get you there unconsciously. As you can see, this is an efficient, energy-saving system when used positively for self-production. When an unconscious habit pattern is destructive to us, we must use our conscious minds to break the habit. Bringing our habitual behavior into conscious awareness is hard work, and so the behavior to be changed must be important enough for us to expend the energy.

The central question which must be asked of oneself is, "How important is it to me to change this behavior now?" If the answer is an unequivocal, "This is the most important thing to do right now," then the rest is fairly simple. If the answer is, "Well there are a number of things I think I should change," then you need to go through the process of sorting out to determine the number one priority item. When you believe that there are a great number of things of equal importance to change, you become overwhelmed. Your feeling of confusion and helplessness inevitably results in your doing nothing rather than focusing on one or a few things and accomplishing them. It appears to be a characteristic of many people to use this defense of confusion to avoid making changes in their lives. The feeling of frustration and hopelessness results in an even greater entrenchment in the "poor me" syndrome, and of course no change is ever forthcoming.

An alternate approach, which results in success, is to decide clearly on one aspect of your behavior that you are going to change. There are probably a number of important issues, but you must force yourself to zero in on one particular item to begin. Once you have established which bit of behavior you are going to change first, then let all of the other problem areas go. Stop giving any thought to the other behavior altogether. Put all your concentrated energy into *the* problem to be solved. For most people the process of sorting out the most significant thing to change first is a difficult task. This is because of the old habit pattern of keeping yourself confused to avoid having to make any change. Remember that choosing one particular behavior and really working on "it" is contradictory to your old pattern and will therefore meet with resistance. Nevertheless, you must forge ahead. Eventually you can get around to the other seemingly important behaviors, but begin by choosing *one* high-priority behavior to change.

Chapter 2

Why Can't You Change?

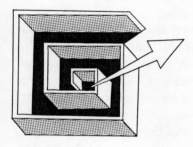

What is stopping you from changing? You are reading this book because there is something you would like to change about yourself. In order to make a change you must look at the ideas or beliefs you have which encourage and perpetuate the problem behavior. In all cases of correctable problem behavior, there is a strongly held belief system which discourages change. Until these beliefs and expectations are modified, the likelihood of significant change is very small.

The most common expression of believed inability to change is found in the word *can't*. *Can't* literally means *cannot* or *is incapable of*. Whenever a person says "I can't," he or she is saying, "I am not capable of doing the behavior in question." For instance, we commonly hear people say, "I'm sorry, I can't have lunch with you," or "I can't make that meeting tonight," or "I can't lose weight." All these statements are untrue. No one is incapable of having lunch with another, but one may *choose* not to for a variety of reasons. Similarly, we are all capable of attending meetings and losing weight, but when we make the "I can't" statements, we have chosen not to. Unfortunately, the word *can't* is used so much that the user begins to believe the incapability and gives up on trying to change. The feeling of incapability becomes strongly ingrained as a permanent part of one's personality. If you pay attention to your speech, you will see that you are using incapability words inappropriately much of the time to get yourself out of doing all sorts of things. This practice also prevents you from seeing yourself as capable of doing many of the things you think you would like to do. This is true of the athlete who believes he or she can't score the goal, and the housewife who believes she can't get out of the house, and the employees who think they can't get promoted. The tendency is to view oneself as incapable, speak to oneself in

terms of "I can't," then continue in patterns of not succeeding, while complaining about it. Until you clearly see that
you are continually reinforcing your inability to change, you
will not be able to turn that inability thinking around into capability thinking.

Each of us has been trained in particular ideas about
ourselves and our abilities. We see ourselves as talented, attractive, smart, skilled, confident, responsible, or whatever
we believe about ourselves. We rarely question these ideas,
even though everything in our environment may be in dis-
agreement with our beliefs.

For instance, Dave, a handsome young man came to me one
day complaining of anxiety and depression. He felt that he was
quite unlovable and that no woman would want to have anything to do with him. Upon exploring his interactions with
women, it was quickly found that he was well liked and respected by many of the women in his office, who frequently
flirted with him and complimented him. Every time one of the
women would approach him, however, he perceived it as "just
playing with him" and denied to himself the fact that they could
actually be serious. He viewed himself as shy and incompetent
in making and maintaining friendships and sought out the company of prostitutes for sexual release. His contact with prostitutes further convinced and reinforced him in his beliefs about
his unattractiveness and worthlessness. With this reinforcement of his beliefs he withdrew into himself more and more until he was consciously avoiding other people and isolating
himself. His rationalization for isolating himself was that he was
afraid of being rejected if he allowed himself to be involved with
anyone. His anticipation of rejection came out of his old beliefs
that he was unworthy and unlovable; he projected these feelings onto those people around him, expecting them to feel the
same way about him that he felt about himself. He had created

a tight, logical system which supported his negative views of himself, and he worked hard every day to maintain his beliefs and expectations.

In therapy, I questioned the validity of the young man's beliefs and demanded proof that he was as worthless and unlovable as he felt. He was instructed to interview at least three persons who knew him and to gain information from them about their perceptions of him. He was, of course, very resistant to asking people what they thought of him, but was faced with the option of either getting the data requested or continuing in the painful depressed state. The following week he returned with information from two fellow employees and a relative. All three agreed that they viewed him as a really nice person who they would like to know better. They acknowledged that they were aware he had been isolating himself more than usual and they were sincerely concerned about him. The young man found it hard to believe that these people would want to know him better or that they were concerned about him. However, the data and proof were before him and in therapy he was forced to fit them into his belief system. In order to make this new information fit, he had to readjust his beliefs to accommodate the new data. Initially he tried to pass it off as just kindness on their part, but I pushed him to either recognize that the world viewed him differently than he viewed himself or go out and collect more data. He didn't want to collect more information so he accepted the fact that other people perceived him differently than he perceived himself. This inroad into his strongly held negative belief about himself was the beginning of the change in his beliefs to fit more closely the person he really was. Within a few months he was interacting more appropriately with people and had the beginnings of a few good relationships. Of course his depression and anxiety had disappeared as he incorporated a more positive view of himself and acted accordingly.

Our beliefs and the behaviors which accompany and support them are incredibly powerful influences in our lives.

Our perceptions of events are influenced more by our beliefs than by the reality of the events. For instance, the extensive research done on the powerful effects of placebos demonstrates clearly the power of beliefs and expectations. A placebo is an inert chemical substance with no inherent ability to do anything. When it is given to a person who believes it is a chemical or medicine that he or she wants or needs, the bodily response is frequently the same as if the real chemical or medicine had been given. The mind is not able to differentiate between what is actually taken in and what is believed to have been taken. The same phenomenon can occur if a person ingests a placebo but believes it is a substance to which he or she is allergic. There are numerous reports of allergic reactions, illnesses, and even death from the ingestion of placebos which were believed to be something else. We can safely say, then, that what you believe can kill you. Fortunately, overt deaths from such experiences are rare, but the pain and suffering incurred from strongly held erroneous beliefs is monumental. Almost all people suffer from some erroneous beliefs about themselves, and these beliefs inhibit their behavior.

To effectively change yourself, you must believe yourself capable of changing and you must have no beliefs which prevent the change. To overcome these powerful negative forces, you must go through an exhaustive critical examination of the ideas, conceptions, and expectations you have about the change in question and ultimately achieve the truth about your real ability to change yourself. The most effective technique is self-examination: you ask yourself, "What proof do I have that I am not capable of making this change?" Begin by listing all of the reasons you can think of why you could not change the behavior up until now. When you have finished the list, go back over it and critically examine these ideas, one by one, demanding proof or falsehood for each belief. It is often helpful to write down any proof you have to maintain a particular idea. Continue to analyze and scrutinize each excuse until you have exhausted the list. A useful mnemonic device for remembering this procedure is:

1. Elicit
2. Examine
3. Erode
4. Exhaust

These are the four E's of changing beliefs. For each behavior you would like to change:

1. Elicit all your ideas about why you do it or feel you can't do it.

2. Examine each one in critical detail, requiring proof and hard data to support the idea.

3. Erode each of the beliefs by the analytical examination.

4. Exhaust all the excuses so that there is nothing left to inhibit or block you from changing.

Once you have gone through this process you will be in a positive position to change because you will no longer have any reasons for maintaining the negative position.

There are literally hundreds of excuses which have been used to avoid making change. Each excuse contains the same basic ingredient: "Because of this, I can't change." Following are some of the most common and popular beliefs and excuses used to avoid change.

Phases or Stages of Life

The idea that a person is just passing through a phase or stage in life is popular with both children and adults. We hear all kinds of behavior excused because a child is in the terrible twos or the tyrannical teens. It is also commonplace to hear behaviors such as bedwetting or soiling excused as just a phase or stage the child is passing through. Unfortunately, many of these behaviors do not change even after the phase is long gone. The same phenomenon occurs in adults. Sometimes the excuse is, "I'm too young to do that," or "I'm too old to get into that sort of thing." Recently a popular phase excuse has been the midlife crisis. Using the midlife excuse, many men have begun cheating on their wives, involving themselves with young girls, and in general trying to behave like teenagers. The result of this kind of behavior is often disastrous to both the man and his family, but no great attempts are made to help the man change; he is excused because, "He is just going through his midlife crisis." There may be some validity to categorizing the phases of adult life. However, there is great danger in accepting these phases as essential and immutable. People are more likely to deny responsibility for changing themselves if they have a socially supported belief or excuse to back them.

Mr. Gross is a 49-year-old prominent business executive and pillar of his community. He has been married for 25 years and has three children, ages 21, 18, and 17. The family has been very involved in the community, active in the church and the yacht club, and outstanding in many social achievements. During the past year, Mr. Gross began drinking much more heavily than ever before and at the same time staying away from his family for longer hours each day. His excuses were increased work pressures but his wife recognized his withdrawal from her and his incipient depression. Mrs. Gross came to me to aid her in helping her husband. She was encouraged to bring her husband into the therapy sessions and ultimately, after great resistance, he did come in with her. He held his position very strongly, stating that there was nothing wrong with him, that the only difference was the increase in work pressure and what he described as the family demanding too much of him at the same time. Mr. Gross agreed to one session alone with me. In this session he clearly described his midlife anxieties and dissatisfaction with his stable, secure family life. He told about several of his friends of approximately the same age who had left their families and gone on to greater happiness and fulfillment with younger women. Mr. Gross had become involved with a 26-year-old secretary in his office and had some preliminary plans to leave his wife and family and move in with her.

I questioned the validity of Mr. Gross's beliefs about his midlife stage and encouraged him to evaluate whether he was really undergoing a psycho-physiological change in himself or was getting caught up in a popular belief system. I also asked him to evaluate his goals and priorities in life and his previously proven methods of attaining them. Mr. Gross agreed to see me again, and further erosion was done on his midlife crisis belief system. By the third session, he could see that he had become somewhat bored with his job and family success and had bought into the midlife crisis belief system as a way out.

He now decided that it was important to stimulate himself and develop some new challenges, but he didn't want to sacrifice his family and friends to accomplish this. He resolved to make some significant changes in his job and he and his wife began some marriage enrichment exercises to bring new life into their relationship. Approximately two months later Mr. and Mrs. Gross announced they would be spending the next two to five years in Europe, where Mr. Gross would be heading a major new project for his company. Both of them were as excited as little children about the challenge and opportunity of the move. As they looked back on their stormy past year, Mr. Gross reflected, "I am really thankful that I was able to get out of my midlife crisis before I believed it so strongly that I couldn't get out. I only wish I could help several of my friends who are ruining their lives, believing that they can't help themselves and must go through the divorce and pain of the midlife crisis."

Hereditary Incapability

How can we possibly be expected to change or overcome something with which we were born? There is very little evidence that there are any behaviors, good or bad, which are genetic. However, the excuse "I can't help it because I was born that way" is a common cop-out for many people. We often look to our parents and excuse our behaviors because we are like them and must have inherited a particular characteristic, ability, or disability. The most common excuse for a bad temper is that it was handed down from one of the parents. More likely, temper tantrums are tolerated and accepted much more in a family where one or both adults enjoy temper tantrums. This is not a hereditary phenomenon but is learned and accepted behavior. Another common hereditary belief is obesity. Often obese people will say that they inherited a tendency to be fat or that they were born with big bones. The belief seems to fit because usually where you find an obese offspring you will find an obese parent. It is quite rare to find two parents who are trim and in good shape who have an obese child. However, is this hereditary, or is it conditioned learning? Many therapists' experience indicates that this kind of behavior has nothing to do with genetics but is purely learned pattern behavior. Some other common genetic disability excuses are, lack of athletic ability, lack of musical talent, shyness, and inability to learn certain subjects like mathematics, history, or English. In each case children are taught by their parents that they are not expected to achieve great success in the areas of believed genetic inability. If the child does poorly in math and his mother also has problems in math, then it is likely that the child will be encouraged not to work harder and achieve but rather to accept the genetic limitations and do poorly. These beliefs become ingrained in each of us and are then a part of our adult personality and inhibit even thoughts of significant change in many areas.

Instinctual Needs

Modern psychology, beginning primarily with Sigmund Freud, has given us a host of psychological excuses for our behaviors. The theoretical constructs of the psychosexual stages of development have been modified by many people to explain their "out of control" behavior. The view is that a person has become fixated in a particular stage of development and manifests behavior appropriate to that stage without being able to modify the behavior significantly. For example, the heavy smoker is often viewed as having very strong oral needs. Frequently the weaning process from the breast or bottle is the target of blame for the adult oral behavior. Of course, as long as a man believes that the primary reason he "needs" to smoke is that he was not properly weaned, he cannot seriously consider stopping smoking, because he believes his powerful instinctual need must be gratified. The same excuse is also used frequently by adults who overeat. These people often describe an insatiable craving for food, feeling deprived, unloved, and depressed if frustrated; the momentary feelings of deprivation are quickly relieved by the presence of some kind of food in the mouth. These people view themselves as out of control in regard to overeating; they frequently refer to the overeating as a compulsion which they cannot consciously control. They call themselves "oral compulsives."

The concept of compulsive behavior is rooted in this instinctual needs belief system. The compulsions are believed to be uncontrollable, unconscious behaviors which relieve anxiety when repeated over and over. There is actually no proof that any such unconscious compulsive behavior exists in human beings. It is not difficult to prove that there is conscious control over every bit of so-called unconscious compulsive behavior. A case example may help to elucidate this fundamental assumption.

Bob Jones was 34 years old when he sought treatment for his voyeurism. He had been peeking in women's bedrooms for seventeen years and had been caught only one time, approximately two weeks after he had begun the behavior. At age 34, Bob was a very successful executive in a large manufacturing plant, recently having been promoted to vice-president of the company. He came to therapy because he felt a conflict between his voyeurism and his status in the community and on the job. Bob had been married for ten years and had no children. He had seen two other therapists. The first was at age 17, after the police caught him peeking in a neighbor's window. Bob's parents took him to a psychiatrist who, after interviewing him, told them that he had a compulsive disorder which would require several years of intensive psychotherapy. Bob's parents could not afford the suggested four day per week analytic treatment, and instead punished Bob and told him that they never wanted to catch him looking in neighbors' windows again. Bob did exactly what his parents demanded: he improved his skills at voyeurism so expertly that he had not been caught again in the ensuing seventeen years. Upon his promotion to vice-president, Bob began to feel more anxious about his voyeurism. He consulted another psychiatrist, who informed him that he was suffering from a compulsive disorder which was very hard to treat but that with the intensive analytic treatment they could probably work it out in three or four years working four to five days per week. Bob was highly motivated to stop his voyeurism, and he sought my opinion before beginning the analytic work.

In the first session I asked him who was in control of the so-called compulsive behavior. Bob responded that he figured he must be but since it was a compulsion he wasn't able to stop it. I questioned in minute detail how this "compulsion" worked. Initially Bob tried to excuse his behavior as just out of his control, but I continued to ask about the details of exactly when an idea to peek started and how Bob worked out the plans so that he did not get caught. Bob related that he looked in women's bedrooms only on Wednesday nights because that was the night he went bowling with his company bowling team. He explained that he would hurry through the bowling and then spend about one hour going from house to house peeking in the windows and masturbating. I asked how he knew which windows to peek in and how he avoided getting caught. He proudly described how he had developed a particular route based on the usual bedtimes of the women he was watching and corresponding to the police car schedule. He had worked out his route with great precision and timing which prevented his being detected. I then asked how this could be compulsive behavior since it seemed that Bob was in excellent control of himself at all times. Bob replied that he just couldn't help himself. I then questioned him in detail about the specifics of his preparation for his voyeuristic adventures. It turned out that Bob would usually begin planning the evening sometime on Wednesday morning, when he would feel stimulated by one of the secretaries in his office. He would take out his up-to-date real estate maps and his current police route schedule from the bottom drawer of his desk and begin to map out his route for that evening. I asked him who was in control of taking those schedules and maps out of the bottom drawer. He answered that he was in control. I asked whether he felt compelled to take out the maps or whether it was by choice. Bob thought and realized that it was completely by conscious choice that he planned the evening's voyeurism. I then suggested that Bob make an overt conscious decision the following Wednesday about whether he really wanted to take out the maps and schedules or leave them in the drawer each time he felt the urge during the day. I also pointed out that he was obviously very good at his voyeurism and therefore had little to fear regarding getting caught and embarrassing himself and his family. Therefore, the conscious choice to continue or discontinue the voyeurism was totally up to Bob, and if he chose to stop it he could by stopping himself in the planning stages, where he knew he was in complete control.

The following week Bob returned, jubilant over his success. For the first time in seventeen years he had gone an entire week without looking in any woman's window. I asked how he had been so successful in stopping the behavior. Bob explained that on Wednesday morning, when he felt stimulated by one of the secretaries, he reached down to take out the maps and schedules but stopped himself as he was opening the drawer. He said he asked himself, "Do I really want to plan this now or shall I choose not to do it right now?" He asked himself the same question every time he felt the urge, and soon it was quitting time and he had not planned his route. He went bowling that evening and, knowing he was not prepared for peeking, bowled better than usual. Bob described this phenomenon as a miracle. I made it clear to him that it was not a miracle but rather that he had made a conscious choice and controlled himself. I also strongly reinforced his ability to control any and all of his behavior and thoroughly eroded the concept that he was suffering from a compulsive disorder. When I saw him two weeks later, he was still successful in controlling his voyeurism. Five weeks after the initial interview, Bob elected to terminate the therapy as he felt completely in control of himself. I contacted Bob one year and two years after he ceased his voyeurism and he reported that there had been no return to that behavior; he felt much better about his life, he was getting along better with his wife, he was more successful on the job, and even his bowling game had significantly improved.

Most of what we feel to be "needs" are actually wishes, desires, and choices. It is very dangerous to believe that you are being controlled by unconscious needs, because then you are not in a position to do anything to change the behavior. No matter what the behavior, ask yourself, "Who is really in charge of my doing this?" The only instinctual needs appear to be for food, water, and oxygen. Beyond the survival needs, everything else is conscious choice.

Emotional Illness

The excuse of being unable to control yourself because you are crazy has become very popular in recent years. The plea of not guilty by reason of insanity has been cleverly used in several famous murder trials to modify the verdict. This kind of irresponsible thinking has spread rapidly. Phrases such as "I just couldn't help myself," or "I must have flipped out and not known what I was doing," or "I was temporarily insane" are being heard more and more to excuse inappropriate behavior. Psychologizing everything has become a national pastime. No matter what the newsworthy event, reporting frequently includes a psychiatrist or psychologist explaining why the events occurred. A criminal's inability to control himself, usually because of mental illness, is often given as the underlying cause of the action. We are bombarded with examples of people getting away with grossly inappropriate, irresponsible behavior because of this. It is not surprising, then, that the excuse of some kind of emotional illness is becoming quite popular.

Emotional illness as an excuse to maintain behavior or avoid changing behavior comes in many forms. Sometimes the form is overt, as in the psychosis. Other times it is covert and harder to pinpoint, expressed in phrases like "I'm just shy," or "that's just my personality," or "that's just the way I am, and I can't help it." In whatever form it takes, behavior is excused and no efforts at change are made. To increase the resistance to change, the associated beliefs surrounding emotional illness are that it is deep-seated, long-standing, deeply rooted, and very hard to change if changeable at all. We hear people say, "I know this is an emotional problem and is rooted deeply in my childhood, so I can't expect it to change overnight." With this kind of a philosophy, there is little chance for change.

One of the most common emotional illness excuses is shyness. The Stanford Shyness Study, reported in *Shyness: What It Is, What to Do About It,* by Philip Zimbardo (Addison-Wesley, Reading, Mass., 1977), shows that approximately 40 percent of the American population consider themselves shy. A total of 80 percent of the people surveyed reported that they were shy at some point in their lives. These statistics make the phenomenon of shyness an epidemic. The extensive research on shyness clearly shows that it is not an emotional illness but a learned way of behaving. Parents who are shy, or were shy as children, either overtly or covertly encourage their children to be shy. Little effort is made to modify the shy behavior because it is viewed as normal, expected, and appropriate during the child's development. Later, when the shyness significantly interferes with the child's or young adult's healthy functioning, it becomes a symptomatic focus and a problem. Unfortunately, like other habit pattern behaviors, shyness often takes on a life of its own and becomes very hard to change because of the years of reinforcement it has received.

Another, even more common, emotional illness belief is depression. It has been estimated that at least 80 percent of people visiting their family doctor with a multitude of organic symptoms are actually suffering from physical manifestations of depression. It is still more acceptable in our society to have a physical illness than an emotional illness. In addition, depression ranks as the leading problem being treated by psychotherapists across the country. We cannot doubt, from these statistics, that many people believe they are depressed. The question is, does depression really exist as a mental illness or is it just another learned way of behaving? My experience suggests that there appear to be a few kinds of experiences which may be viewed as "real" depressions and which are primarily out of the conscious control of the suffering person. One of these is the depressive phase of a manic-depressive psychosis. Evidence suggests that manic-depressive psychosis is probably a hereditary biochemical phenomenon. There are other psychotic depressions which are felt to be beyond the person's control, but we do not have hard data regarding these depressions. It is likely that they are actually an extreme extension of the so-called neurotic depressions. The possibility that there is a biochemical change associated with the severe psychotic depressions is also likely, since usually a person has been suffering with the problem for a long time and has probably readjusted his or her brain biochemistry accordingly.

Learning to behave in a depressed manner is very easy in our society. Our parenting strategies are primarily concerned with punishment, reprimands, and put-downs. We spend very little time or energy reinforcing the positive in our children. Children quickly learn that they get more love and attention for being "bad" than for being good. Therefore, many children persist in bad behaviors which force their parents to interact with them. They experience all the negative feelings and words from their parents and begin to incorporate these into the idea of who they really are. It doesn't take long before a child fully agrees with his parents that he is basically bad. This bad feeling may be expressed in angry, aggressive misbehavior, or it may come out in withdrawal and isolation. Thus the underlying feeling of badness gets translated as depression. Once the strong negative-self feelings get firmly rooted, they are perpetuated by behaviors consistent with a negative self-view. This cycle of feelings and behaviors spirals the victim deeper and deeper until the point of loss of control is reached. In the majority of persons, the negative-self feelings do not reach the severe, out-of-control proportion. These people go through life feeling down much of the time and feeling that life isn't much fun for them. Unfortunately, they rarely look within themselves for change but wait for the outside world to make them feel better. Since the problem is 100 percent within them, they are consistently disappointed and reinforced in their negative position. One can easily see how this pattern gets developed and reinforced. The question is how to break out of it.

Remember that it is the beliefs and expectations which keep the behavior going. Go through the process of examining and critically analyzing each belief and proving its validity or falsehood. Just because a person behaves in a depressed fashion does not mean that person is depressed. Ask yourself, "How do I really know for sure that I am depressed?"

"What evidence do I have that I am depressed?" "Can I prove that I am depressed or have I just been believing so and acting accordingly?" "Are there times when I do not act depressed?" Force yourself to come up with data to confirm or deny your position.

Medical Problems

During the course of a lifetime it is likely that each person will contract a certain number of diseases, have a number of accidents, and be involved in medical treatments of various kinds. These are very real experiences and sometimes change the course of one's life. A danger of medical problems is that they can be very reinforcing, gratifying experiences in changing one's behavior and the behavior of loved ones. It has been shown that sick persons get touched and attended to significantly more than when they are healthy. Our loved ones tend to go out of their way to be nice to us, give us gifts, and spend much more time with us when we are sick. It is only reasonable, then, that a significant number of people make an unconscious connection between sick and being loved and cared for. These people tend either to have a series of diseases through much of their life or to develop chronic diseases which get better or worse but are always present. The gains which they received initially are often lost, but, like other behavior patterns, these persist because at one time they succeeded in bringing gratification.

With any kind of medical illness which inhibits or impairs functioning, the central question to be asked is: "Does this condition absolutely prevent me from doing what I want to do or can I find a way to do it in spite of this illness?" Beware of assumptions which suggest that you are incapable of doing (can't do) something just because you have a certain condition. Make yourself prove, beyond any other possibility, that what you want to do is absolutely 100 percent impossible in your condition. If you have this *proof*, then you can relax and plan alternatives. If you do not have proof, then begin to make plans for how you are going to make it happen.

Joe Harrington is a good example of how this process works with a serious medical disease.

Joe was 15 years old when he came to me with problems of school failure, truancy, and marijuana use. Joe's parents were deeply concerned because he had always been an A student and had had no previous trouble in school. Joe's excuse about why he was cutting school, failing, and using marijuana was that he felt like a freak with his artificial left leg. At age 6 Joe had developed a rare bone tumor of his lower left leg and had an amputation below the knee. He had been fitted with an excellent artificial limb and had done very well adjusting to his condition up to this time in high school. Now Joe stated he was being teased because of his limp and felt that he didn't fit in with the rest of the students. In grade school Joe had been very active in sports and was especially fond of swimming. Joe felt he wasn't good enough to compete in high school. He assumed that he would be rejected if he tried, so he didn't bother to try.

I questioned the validity of Joe's disability and the facts regarding his ability to swim. It turned out Joe was an excellent swimmer with a certificate in lifesaving. I encouraged him to talk with the swim team coach to determine if his medical disability would keep him off the team. The coach gave Joe a tryout and immediately signed him up for the water polo team. One year later Joe received an award as the outstanding water polo player of the year and was elected captain of the team. The problems of school failure, truancy, and drugs were no longer present.

This example underscores the common phenomenon of using a medical condition as an excuse to avoid doing something of which you are truly capable. Remember to scrutinize any and all beliefs before you accept them as fact and act on them.

Chronological Age

An amazing number of people use their age as a reason for not doing something. They are either too young or too old. Our society has encouraged age-related beliefs by putting restrictions on people based on their age. There is an age when you are allowed to drive, drink, get married, and retire. Unfortunately, the assumption has been made that the legal age and chronological age have something to do with maturity and capability. It is very evident that that is not the case. Age is an arbitrary designation attached to each of us which should not interfere with any of our functioning. Nevertheless, too often age is used as an excuse to avoid new behaviors, challenging behaviors, or behaviors that are significantly different from the usual patterns. The result is maintenance of the same old patterns day after day, accompanied by boredom, apathy, and depression. These people, no matter what age, are classified as the "living dead." They don't take on any risks or challenges, but bask in the apparent comfort of old patterns. These same people often complain about how dull life is and how the rest of the world seems to be having so much fun while they continue in daily misery. They rarely see that it is themselves who must change if they are to experience anything new and bring new life into their lives. No matter what chronological age you are, ask yourself what evidence you have that you can or cannot do what you want to do. Is it your age that is stopping you or is it your beliefs that your age is stopping you?

Environment

The idea of environmental influence on people's behavior became very popular in the 1970's. Overcrowding, pollution, excessive heat or cold, fluorescent lights, chemical preservatives and dyes, and the other humans around us are being studied to determine their effects on our feelings and behavior. There is significant indication that many of these phenomena do influence our behaviors, but we must be extremely careful not to indulge ourselves in environmental excuses which truly do not exist.

A very common case in point is the parent of an active child. Often the first thought is that the child is hyperactive from eating too much sugar, food dyes, preservatives, etc. While the parent is focusing on the external environmental causes, the parent-child interaction is being avoided. If a mother can convince herself that it is sugar which makes her child behave badly, then the only interaction she needs to have with him is to help him avoid sugar. It certainly would not be reasonable to take a more demanding stand as a parent if you believe it is the environmental factor which must be changed. People who fall into the environmental trap often allow gross misbehavior to continue for years while they pursue environmental causes to explain such behaviors. They totally avoid demanding the behavior change because they believe it cannot change as long as the environmental stimulus is present.

An example from my practice will illustrate the devastating effects such belief systems can have.

Peggy was a 34-year-old single woman when she first visited me. She complained of isolation, depression, insomnia, loss of appetite, and multiple body aches and pains. From her history it appeared she spent most of her time in doctors' offices. She was being treated for multiple allergies to foods, dust, dander, pollens, etc., as well as for chronic unexplained pain in her abdomen, frequent severe headaches, and general malaise and fatigue. Peggy was absolutely convinced that her problems were all related to various allergies and she had spent most of her life going from doctor to doctor trying various special diets and injections to free herself from this life of misery. She usually received some minor relief each time she tried a new program but she had never found anything that lasted for her.

A bit of Peggy's history helps one to understand her current dilemma. Peggy was born prematurely with a birth weight of 4 pounds, 6 ounces. She was very sickly as an infant and child and was treated primarily for allergies to various foods. Her symptoms as a small child were not much relieved by the long course of allergy shots and the severe limitation of what she could eat. She spent endless hours in doctors' offices and at home in bed with her mother caring for her. Her illnesses caused her to miss a great deal of school, but with the help of tutors and her own innate intelligence she graduated from high school. Unfortunately, she missed most of the normal adolescent social interaction; she had no real friends and was not involved in any of the usual high school social activities. At age 34 she had had only a few dates and was still a virgin. She lived alone in an apartment near her parents' home and spent many evenings and weekends with them. She avoided any social interactions outside her family for fear of developing an allergic attack. She refused to go out to restaurants because she believed the food might be contaminated by preservatives or contain substances which would make her ill. Peggy worked as an assistant accountant and had only a very casual relationship with the other employees, although several had tried to encourage her to do things with them. Peggy's primary excuse for avoiding the world was that she believed she was allergic to almost everything in the world and needed to avoid it to stay alive. Yet she was barely existing in her current status and was certainly not alive in any meaningful sense.

I offered Peggy deep relaxation and self-hypnosis to assist her in overcoming her handicap. Initially she responded very well and controlled her headaches and the pain in the abdomen. Using the deep-relaxation, self-control techniques, Peggy avoided allergy attacks for four weeks and even took the chance of having lunch at a health food restaurant with a colleague from the office. On her fifth visit to me, Peggy explained that she was terminating treatment because her parents felt the self-hypnosis was unnatural and dangerous. She said that they were going to a new allergy specialist 500 miles away and she was hopeful that he might be able to give her some relief. Peggy had done well using her own natural abilities to help herself, but she claimed that she felt uncomfortable using the relaxation techniques and much preferred the treatments she received from allergy doctors. Unfortunately, because of her own and her parents' beliefs, Peggy continues to suffer unnecessarily even after proving to herself that she is capable of changing herself and that it is not the environment causing all her problems.

In all of the examples in this chapter the message is the same. Behavior does not change until the beliefs are changed or at least seriously doubted. As long as the excuses for the behavior are present, there is no reason to expect any behavior to change. Seriously questioning and scrutinizing beliefs results in getting to the actual facts regarding ability or inability. Once these assumptions are cleared away, then action can be taken and behavior changed. Nothing changes as long as it has support to stay the same.

Chapter 3

How Not To Get Yourself To Do What You Want To Do

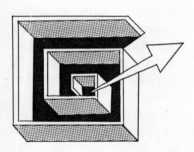

Whenever people want to change something about themselves, they frequently have stories of numerous unsuccessful attempts. It is quite rare to hear of someone trying to change a particular behavior for the first time. Much more commonly we hear of how many fruitless attempts have been made, with the behavior persisting. A very good example is the problem of overweight. Every one of the several hundred obese persons I have treated had tried an assortment of diets, exercise programs, pills, shots, and special reducing garments. In all cases, these attempts were unsuccessful and the person was now preparing for another go at it. The same phenomenon is seen in all repetitive pattern behaviors which people think they want to change. The attempts which are made to change the behavior are often revealing about the motivation to change.

Inherent in the concept of change is the idea that something will actually be different. Notice how different this is from someone's trying to change. In the latter case, actual change does not take place but rather a process supposedly aimed at changing is taking place. There is a built-in conflict between actually changing and being in the process of change. A person cannot do both at the same time. If we continue in the process of changing (attempting or making an effort) then we are necessarily avoiding actually making the change. On the other hand, when we actually change a behavior we cannot be in the process since the act is already accomplished. There is a very important distinction between getting what you think you want and working toward getting what you want. A simple example is the habit pattern of smoking cigarettes. Many persons supposedly decide to change their smoking habits. We often hear, "I'm going to try to stop smoking" or "I'm making an effort to cut down on my smoking." In both cases, there is no communication to stop smoking, but rather a clear message to continue but perhaps modify it a bit. The person who clearly decides to stop smoking usually does it with a self-communication such as "I am going to stop smoking today and never smoke again." This is not a process statement, but rather a definitive action statement, and it commonly brings good results.

It is very important to look at the attempts you have made in the past to change yourself and see why they have not worked. Did you fail because you were not capable of changing or did you fail because you excused yourself with a myriad of beliefs and then fooled yourself into thinking you were making change when you were actually maintaining the problem behavior. This distinction between real change and attempts or efforts to change is often very subtle but it is deadly. To be effective and achieve real change you must become conscious of how you are communicating to yourself and realize whether you want to be in the process of change or actually change. The difference is about the same as thinking about eating an ice cream cone or actually eating it. No matter how long you think about the event, nothing happens until you actually make a decision, put your mind and body in motion, and make it happen.

Self-Communications

The actual words that we say to ourselves reveal a great deal about our motivation and/or desire to change. Most people pay little attention to things they say to themselves; they interpret what they are saying to mean something else. These people communicate to others in essentially the same manner, making assumptions that the listeners will somehow figure out what they mean. A frequently heard example is, "Gee, I really would like to get together with you and I'll try to stop by soon." The real message in this communication is, "I don't really care very much if I see you or not." This real message becomes clear as the weeks and months pass by and the communicator avoids appearing. If the listener pays close attention to the words, she will know that the communicator has little intention of stopping by. Unfortunately, many people do not pay close attention to the real words, and then their feelings get hurt by the ensuing behavior. These kinds of communications are often dismissed as small talk or "polite conversation" but they become problematic when used with someone who listens carefully or when used with yourself. The results are often disappointment and a feeling of being let down by someone else or by yourself. In this section we will look carefully at the real words which we communicate and see how they affect our behaviors. In almost all cases, the real words spoken are quite different from what we think we are saying. Some of the most frequent examples of this kind of communication are the following:

Inability

Phrases like "I can't," "I never could," and "I don't think I can," all suggest inability. They mean that the person speaking is not capable of the behavior in question. Usually the actual capability is present, but the speaker is using this phrase to avoid the behavior. For instance, someone might say, "I can't stop smoking" or "I just can't meet you for lunch today." Now, we all know that any person capable of starting smoking is also capable of stopping smoking. It may be difficult for many people, but it is certainly not in the realm of inability.

The same is obviously true of one's ability to have lunch with another. No one is incapable of having lunch with another person; a more honest statement would be that one chooses not to. When we use inability phrases we are avoiding saying what we really mean. When you communicate this kind of information to yourself you perpetuate the problem behavior by creating another unconscious excuse for it. Interestingly, if you say "I can't" to yourself long enough, you will begin to believe it and make it happen.

A common example of long-range effects of "I can't" thinking is the development of public speaking fears. Initially a person is required, usually in grade school, to speak in front of the class. He prepares the material and practices but feels the normal anxiety associated with any public presentation. In the next step he begins to talk to himself about not being able to do it. He often works himself into such a state of fear and anxiety that he avoids presenting the talk by being sick that day. If forced to present the talk, he may stumble through it and fulfill the prophecy. Of course, from then on any threat of public speaking becomes awesome and fearful: he knows he can't do it and then worries and develops ways to avoid the task. As time goes on this fear becomes greater, often to the point where it is destructive to a career. Looking back at the development, we can see that it all began with the belief and feeling of "I can't" or "I'm not able."

Questions

The most frequent communication to self or others regarding behavior is asking a question about it. Such phrases as, "Why did I do that?" "I wonder how long I am going to do this?" "I wonder what is wrong with me that makes me do this?" or

"Why don't I stop this?" all encourage the behavior to continue. Questions are one of the greatest intellectual traps that we have at our disposal for perpetuating behaviors. Most of us delight in trying to analyze in deepest detail the causes of our behaviors. What is frequently overlooked is the paradox of questioning.

When you ask a question, you do not anticipate any behavioral change, you expect some kind of answer. The paradox is, in order to get answers to your questions you must continue to be involved in the behavior so that the behavior can be questioned. For instance, suppose you ask the question "Why do I smoke cigarettes?" In order to answer the question you must smoke cigarettes and examine why you believe you are doing it. If you cease smoking cigarettes it would not make any sense to ask yourself why you are smoking them since you would not be smoking them. You could only review past history of why you used to smoke cigarettes. The same concept is true of all questions. In order for you to arrive at answers to questions, the behavior must be present to analyze. One cannot answer questions about behavior that does not exist.

Sometimes it is certainly useful to ask questions of yourself about your behaviors. An understanding of motives and circumstances, through examination, is occasionally helpful to get a different perspective on a situation and achieve some insight into the behavior. However, all too frequently we get caught up in the intellectual trap of searching for the deep meaning or psychological roots of our behavior, and thereby avoid changing the behavior. This method of dealing with problem behaviors has become especially popular at this time when it is believed that there is some psychological explanation for everything. There is strong support from the media and our friends to dig into the causes of our behaviors rather than change them. You must make a decision: do you want answers, insight, and understanding, or do you want behavioral change?

Wishes and Desires

Another way we speak to ourselves is in the form of wishes and desires. We say, "I wish I had more money," "If only I could lose ten pounds I would be really happy," or "I hope I will be able to meet someone nice to share my life." This kind of wishful thinking worked very well for Dorothy in *The Wizard of Oz* but it doesn't work to change our lives today. Wishes are like inability and questions in that they prevent you from taking any action but provide a subtle feeling that in making the wish or desire you have actually achieved the goal. With this feeling, the pressure of actually having to do anything differently is somewhat relieved and you can settle back and passively wait for something to happen. Unfortunately, wishes and desires rarely come true without significant action on the part of the wisher. Listen carefully to how you are speaking to yourself and pay attention to whether you are using the words *wish, want, desire,* or *hope,* or are you using action words like *will, going to,* or *do.* Substituting the action words in the previous examples you can see the big difference in the meaning: "I am going to have more money," "I will lose ten pounds and I will be happy," and "I am going to meet someone nice to share my life." Although this may seem like just a semantic difference, there is a great deal of evidence to show that the real words you use have an enormous influence over the outcome of events in your life. What you say is what you get.

Explanations and Understanding

Trying to understand or explain why we have certain behaviors is much more popular than working at changing the
behaviors. The reason for this is obvious: understanding requires only a thought process whereas making a change in
behavior requires some definitive action. People have a pro-
pensity to take the easy way out, and thinking is easier than
doing. It is also much less risky. Therefore, rather than developing a plan of action to change ourselves, we frequently
tell ourselves that we need to understand why we are having
the problem before we can change it. Unfortunately, there
has been a great deal of support given to this belief by modern
Freudian psychology with its emphasis on insight and understanding. In reality, very few people ever change their behaviors through gaining insight into the causes of their behavioral patterns. Numerous studies by behavioral psychologists
and psychiatrists have shown that behavioral change rarely
follows insight. In fact, frequently the opposite phenomenon
occurs. Following significant behavioral change, many people
experience insight into why they were engaging in the problem behavior. The reason for this phenomenon appears
quite simple. When you are deeply enmeshed in your long-
term habitual problem behavior, it is nearly impossible to see
and understand yourself clearly. After you are no longer
caught up in the problem behavior, then you can clearly see
why you were doing it. It is much like the problem of not being able to see the forest for the trees. When you are in the
middle of the forest you can only see the trees (small problems) with no comprehension of the entire forest (big behavioral pattern). When you rise above the forest and can see the
whole picture clearly, then you can see how the individual

parts fit together to make up the whole. When we stop a behavioral pattern or change it, we get some distance from it and can look back and understand why we were doing it in the first place.

You must be very careful in listening to yourself to see whether you are looking for understanding and explanations or whether you are after behavioral change. If you find yourself asking over and over, "I wonder why I continue doing this" or "If I only understood the deep psychological roots of this behavior then I could change," beware. Grab hold of yourself and realize that you are avoiding change by playing the insight game. As a no-risk experiment, pick some fairly small problem behavior and make an arbitrary decision to change or stop the behavior consistently for two weeks. Make notes in a diary of the insight or understanding which comes to you about that old behavior once you have ceased doing it. With long-standing habit patterns, the length of time away from the behavior required to get the understanding is usually four to six weeks. I am not suggesting that insight and understanding are not useful, but they are not the steps leading to behavioral change. Remember that insight follows change, change does not necessarily follow insight.

Classification or Self-Labeling

Another communication to ourselves which is an expression of avoidance of behavioral change is classifying or labeling ourselves. The greatest disadvantage of this communication is the damage it does to our self-esteem, since it perpetuates the negative or unsuccessful problem behavior. We commonly say things such as, "I can't do it because I'm depressed," "I'm just not good-looking enough to meet someone really nice," or "I'm just basically bad or sick." Each of these communications prevents any kind of change of behavior, and at the same time the message influences our view of ourselves. Such continual negative communications result in a strong belief that we fit these labels, and of course we behave accordingly. This kind of self-communication tends to generalize to many areas of our lives and frequently results in an inhibition of much successful behavior. As we continue to behave unsuccessfully, we reinforce the negative self-view and bind ourselves up in a strong negative downward spiral which often ends in serious depression, withdrawal, and occasionally suicide.

Examine the words you are saying to yourself and watch for labels or classifications. Listen carefully for words like *fat, ugly, dumb, stupid, incompetent, failure, jerk, slob,* and so on. When you hear yourself using these labels about yourself, stop yourself immediately and ask for the evidence to support the label. Maybe the behavior you just did was dumb or foolish but that does not make *you* dumb or a fool. Remember that all of the problem behaviors are just old habits and can be changed. The bad habits are not who you are, they are just things you have learned to do. Each of us is much more than the sum of our behaviors. Unfortunately, the people around us, and we ourselves, tend to judge us on what we do and in time we assume that what we do is who we are. Be careful not to make this equation between what you do and who you are. This association can be deadly if you are caught up in a number of rotten habits; you can only view yourself as rotten, even though no one is rotten or bad basically.

Even if you have developed a strong negative self-view over a long time with many associated negative labels, you can begin to help yourself by questioning those labels, laughing at yourself for continuing to use them, then changing them into positive labels. For instance, if you make a mistake doing something, and catch yourself calling yourself stupid, stop yourself in that thought and say, "Wait a minute, I'm not stupid or dumb, I just wasn't paying attention and I made a mistake." Every time that you correct yourself and undo the negative label, you will be working toward turning yourself around into the capable positive person you really are. Because this is a long-standing pattern for most people, it is not going to change radically the first time you do it. However, with enough repititions you will really begin to feel the difference.

Predictions

Many times labels and classifications become so much a part of our thinking that they become predictions for our future. We anticipate that what we have made happen in the past will happen to us in the future. We tend to set up circumstances to ensure that we will continue to experience the same problems and failures that we have always known. This kind of predictability has a certain built-in security, even though the experiences may be consistently negative. It is very much like the comfort of an old pair of shoes. Even though the old ones are worn out, we avoid getting new shoes because we are so accustomed to the old ones. We avoid taking risks because there is the element of unpredictability and we can't be sure of the outcome.

Words that are used to maintain the behavior are, "I've never done well at meeting new people so I know I won't be successful this time either," "I expect I will fail this test," or "I know I won't have fun on this vacation because I never really enjoy myself." There are literally hundreds of predictions we put on ourselves which significantly influence the outcome of our experiences. Predictions tend to perpetuate themselves because we believe them and act accordingly.

Use the same method to change your behavior regarding predictions that you used with labels and classifications. Ask yourself what evidence you have for the validity of the predictions. Examine carefully your beliefs about the predictive statements you communicate to yourself, and prove to yourself their truth or falsehood. In most cases predictions are based on previous negative experiences or no experience at all. We just assume that we wouldn't be able to do something, that we wouldn't like something, or that something negative will happen if we risk a new behavior. Sometimes predictions are rooted in superstitions, like "Bad things will happen to me on Friday the thirteenth," or "My horoscope says this is going to be a bad week for me." These messages have as much power in determining our behavior as we give them. In choosing to change your behavior you must make yourself consciously aware of predictive statements you make to yourself and undermine them. The next time you catch yourself making an assumption about the outcome of an event in your life, question the facts you have to support your assumption and consider assuming the opposite. For instance, if you find yourself assuming that you will be uncomfortable at a party, take a chance and tell yourself over and over that you are going to have fun, meet new people, and truly enjoy yourself. The old predictions of doom will try to sneak into your thoughts, but continue to banish them and replace them with positive, successful assumptions. Amazingly, you will experience a significant change in your behavior when you change your assumptions and predictions.

Shoulds and Oughts

Shoulds and oughts are the great guilt trips we put on our-selves. They cause much unnecessary pain and agony throughout life. Our parents teach us to know right from wrong, and that awareness is important in everyone's development. Unfortunately, they also usually teach us hundreds of shoulds and oughts which are not so valuable: "You should always eat everything on your plate," "You ought to stay married for the sake of the children," "You should always be sweet and kind no matter what happens." In each case we experience guilt and an internal sense of failure when we don't do what we should do. Much of the time the shoulds and oughts are totally inappropriate for your current life circumstances but the nagging guilt feelings remain. These prohibitions are very effective in controlling behavior through guilt. The element that is left out is the factor of personal choice and self-control. When we respond only to what we should do, we are negating our ability to make a personal choice based on our own unique experience and current life. The result is a subtle feeling of not being in control of one's life, a feeling that can lead to apathy, helplessness, and depression.

Pay close attention to your real words to yourself and see how many shoulds and oughts you are putting on your-self. Next, pick a few of these shoulds and oughts and ask yourself, "Why should I?" Make yourself take responsibility for the decision to do or not do the behavior, and then give yourself credit for making the decision. There may be many shoulds which you will convert into "I choose to," but there will also be many which you can choose not to accept. Making the personal choice and acting on it gives us a sense of ac-

47

complishment which helps build our positive self-esteem. Continuing to do things because you should puts you in the category of a robot without self-control and diminishes positive self-feelings. The more you take personal responsibility for your life and make decisions and choices based on current available data, the better you will feel about yourself and the more successful you will be.

Chapter 4

Knowing What You Do Right

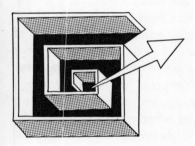

No matter how many problems or failures a person has encountered in his life, he has also experienced many successes. We often overlook the successes because we become preoccupied with our problems and failures. Unfortunately, our society places a greater emphasis on failures and what people do wrong than on success and what people do right. Probably this is best illustrated in the media coverage of news. You can pick up any newspaper or tune into any radio or television news program and see that newsworthy items are people problems and failures. We rarely spend time talking about accomplishments or positive events. Therefore, we all become accustomed to emphasizing the negative aspects of our lives and ignoring the positive. I have asked hundreds of people what they do well in their lives, and the usual response is nothing or very little. Yet upon further questioning I can always elicit examples of competent, successful behavior from these people. The real issue is perspective on one's life; we must learn to go against society's strong negative expectation and search out the positives and successes in each experience. No one has a life full of problems and failures. In every case there are examples of success.

A few years ago Bill, a middle-aged man, came to me because he was severely depressed, feeling his entire life was a failure. He related that everything he had ever attempted or done in his life had always turned out poorly, and now he was contemplating suicide, but he was convinced that he had little chance of succeeding at killing himself since he was so consistently unsuccessful at everything. He had lost his job and family due to alcoholism and could find nothing positive in his life. I questioned him in depth but could not find any significant positive experiences. Finally, I realized that this man's greatest success was his phenomenal ability to set himself up for failure. It became quite clear that he worked day and night to make sure that he always failed at everything he did. On being questioned about each circumstance at work and at home, he gave details of how the successful sabotage was accomplished in each event. This man's failure was no accident. He was incredibly clever at making sure he was never successful at anything except failure, and in failure he was 100 percent successful. When this gentleman saw that he had been so successful all of his life making sure that he failed, he had a new way of viewing himself. With this new perspective on his ability, he was able to turn himself around and use his abilities for success rather than failure.

There are many people who set themselves up for failure in both subtle and overt ways. Few are as extreme as the case above, but the process is the same. The truth is that everyone is capable of success and everyone is successful most of the time. In this section we will analyze successful experiences and see how they occur. Neither success nor failure are accidents: we make them happen.

To examine the essence of your successful behavior, first make a list of the things you do that you really want to do. These may be in such areas as education, recreation, family, job, achievements, and even doing nothing. Ask yourself, "What do I do that I really enjoy and want to do?" If you think you don't have anything in your life that you do because you want to, then you are fooling yourself. Most of us spend considerable time doing things we think we should do, but we also spend time doing what we personally want to do. You must continue to probe your current life experience and come up with your personal list of choice behaviors. It may even include things like smoking, drinking, taking drugs, being "irresponsible," or acting crazy. These are particularly good examples of choice behavior that frequently other people do not want us to engage in.

Once you have your list of choice behaviors, start to examine your ideas and beliefs about these behaviors. In all cases, you will find that you have ideas, expectations, and excuses that allow you to have the behavior. There is no negative, I can't, or I am incapable of doing it thinking. You give yourself permission to do the things you want to do, and you support that permission with a belief that you can do it. This is positive, successful thinking even if the behavior is negative and self-destructive. An outstanding characteristic of people is that they must have a cognitive system or set of beliefs in order to have or not have a particular behavior. There is very little that anyone does without some thinking or reasoning to support his or her behavior. As we saw in earlier chapters, it is these beliefs which allow us to do things or prevent us from doing them. For each item on your list of successful choice behaviors, you have beliefs that tell you it is all right to do it. The ideas may not be logical, rational, or reasonable, but you nevertheless must have them in order to act. In examining the ideas which support your successful behaviors, give special attention to the concept of your capability of doing the behavior. Look at how you convince yourself that it is all right to do it.

The next step in examining your successful behaviors is to look at the techniques you use to accomplish the behaviors in question. Consider how you set up the circumstances to ensure your success, and examine how you overcome obstacles that might prevent your success. Particularly note how you talk to yourself about these behaviors. You give yourself permission, support the permission with ideas which make the behavior acceptable, and finally make positive statements to yourself about being capable and able to engage in the behavior. You will see that you are using strong positive language to yourself to support your behavior. You are not questioning yourself and asking for the deep psychological meaning of why you are doing this. You are not just wishing and hoping that you could do it but are taking a firm stand that you are going to do it. In addition, it is doubtful that you are emphasizing understanding this behavior or classifying or labeling yourself as incapable of doing the behavior in any way. There may be some guilt traces of shoulds and oughts but these are quickly dismissed in favor of going ahead and acting on the desire to do the behavior.

In summary, when we are engaged in successful behavior we make up our minds that it is important for us to do it, then we establish ideas and beliefs to support the behavior. Next we use techniques which we know will get us what we want and we communicate to ourselves that we are capable and deserving of engaging in this behavior. The result is successful choice behavior.

Some of the best examples of successful choice behavior are things we frequently do that we think we don't want or like to do. For example, many people complain about their jobs and say they hate to go to work, yet most people continue to go to work regularly and do a pretty good job. You might say that if you didn't go to work you couldn't eat or have any of the other things you wanted in life, so it's really not a choice. Actually, it is a choice. Each person has complete freedom to choose how they wish to spend each day. No one demands that anyone go to work or produce any products. Most of us choose to go to work, earn money, and spend it as we like. If we look carefully at our communications to ourselves, we often see that we demand of ourselves that we go to work, and we build an elaborate conceptual idea system to support why we need to do this behavior. None of us goes to work without these beliefs that we really need to do it. If you look at the other perspective, you can quickly see that we are making the choice in each step along the way and ultimately achieve the success of going to work and getting what we want.

Another example of clear choice behavior is cigarette smoking. None of us smokes because we have to, but rather by choice. We make up our minds that we want to smoke, despite the protestations of friends, family, and doctors. We find ways to justify the smoking to ourselves: it helps me relax; it calms me down; I like the taste of smoke; I like having a cigarette in my hand; smoking makes me feel better. We dismiss or deny the fact that smoking is dangerous to our health, and substitute ideas such as: people who get lung cancer probably have a family history of it; what is true for laboratory animals is not true for me; you have to die from something, so why not get the enjoyment that you can out of life. We never question our ability to smoke but communicate to ourselves that we enjoy it and can smoke all we want. We prove this by smoking heavily and convincing ourselves that we are enjoying it. Although you may have never viewed cigarette smoking as successful choice behavior, you can see that it is a good example of getting yourself to do what you want to do.

Chapter 5

How to Confront Your Problem and Change

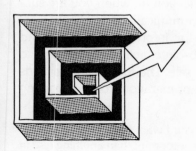

We have now prepared the way for confrontation with yourself. In confronting yourself you put together all of the information you have gained and show yourself either that you are capable of doing what you want to do, or that you are not actually capable of doing what you want to do. In either case you are clear, often for the first time, about exactly where you stand. In most cases the experience of really understanding and feeling oneself as completely capable or absolutely incapable is a truly new experience. Once you have sorted through what you want to do, what your feelings are about it, and what your beliefs are about the behavior, and once you have examined your communications to yourself, then you are in a clear position to either change or maintain your behavior. In addition you have looked at what steps you have taken to change and what things you have done successfully. You have also carefully examined what you do when you are successful in your beliefs, ideas, communications, and behavior.

The next step is to put all this information together and confront yourself with your absolute ability or inability to achieve what you want for yourself. The following questions are useful to ask yourself in preparation for confronting yourself:

1. What is the exact, specific behavior I want to change? Is changing this behavior right now more important than anything else in my life?
2. What evidence do I have that I am capable of making this change? Have I ever done it before? Have I ever successfully accomplished any behavior similar to what I want to do now?
3. What are the reasons and excuses that I have been using to avoid change and to maintain my position regarding this behavior? Do I have real evidence that my reasons are valid, or are they just assumptions?

4. Do I really need to change? What are the advantages of changing over staying just the way I am? Am I willing to do whatever I have to do to change myself?
5. What have I been saying to myself which has prevented me from changing? Is this self-communication accurate or false?

Use a paper and pencil and answer the above questions as precisely as you can. The experience of writing things down is often more powerful and clarifying than just thinking about them. Work hard at answering each question in as much detail as possible. Be careful to avoid in your answers any assumptions or unclear words which will allow you to slip back into old habit patterns. The following example may serve to clarify this process.

Jack Ray is a 43-year-old five foot, six inch, 350-pound man who came to me with complaints of obesity, high blood pressure, early signs of diabetes, and an overall feeling of fatigue. In the initial session he was asked, "Why are you here and what do you want to change?" Mr. Ray responded, "I want to go on a diet." I questioned this huge man, "To gain or lose weight?" "Why to lose, of course," replied Mr. Ray. I responded: "There is no valid assumption that someone wishes to lose weight when they say they want to go on a diet. Diets come in three varieties; to gain, maintain, or lose weight. I would guess that you have been on many diets and have lost many pounds." "Oh yes, I have probably lost over a thousand pounds during my life but I always seem to gain it back somehow," said Mr. Ray. "Well," I questioned, "why should this time be any different from all the rest? Why is it so important right now that you lose weight, and even if you lose it, it sounds like you will just gain it back again anyhow, so why bother?" Mr. Ray replied, "My wife and my doctor think I should lose at least 150 pounds or they

57

say I will endanger my health." I responded, "You probably are endangering your health, and I can understand your wife and doctor's concerns, but how important is it for *you* to lose weight and keep it off?" "Well, I figure you've got to die from something and I really enjoy eating, but I would like to lose weight and keep it off," said Mr. Ray. I replied: "I can assure you that you will not be successful in losing weight and keeping it off until you make a total body decision and commitment. This means that losing whatever number of pounds you desire and maintaining that loss has to be more important to you than anything else in the world. Once you feel that strongly and are one hundred percent committed to change, you will be successful." Mr. Ray pondered what I had said and responded, "Well I can see what you are saying and I think I would like some time to think it over if it requires that kind of commitment."

The following week Mr. Ray returned and proudly announced he had lost ten pounds. I questioned, "Why did you lose ten pounds?" Mr. Ray replied, "I've decided I'm going to try to lose some weight." "I see," I said. "You are planning on doing the same thing this time that you have done every other time. You are going to try, or make attempts, to lose a few pounds, then you will of course gain them back. When you said, 'I am going to try to lose some weight,' you were doing the same thing you have always done, which leaves any commitment or decision out of the communication to yourself. You therefore do not actually have to do anything in order to be successful. In the end you will be able to say you really *tried* but it didn't work and you can go on, obese, believing that there is nothing else you can do. To work with me, you must make a total body commitment either for or against weight loss and maintenance. I will not accept trying or effort-making in place of commitment."

Mr. Ray was surprised at my strong position and stated, "Do you mean that when I say I am going to try to lose weight I am actually letting myself off the hook because there is no real commitment in it?" "Exactly" I said. "Whenever you use the *try* word you are building in an option to fail. You are not committing yourself to success, as you would be if you said, 'I'm going to lose 100 pounds and keep it off.'" Mr. Ray responded, "I can see what you are saying and you are right. I have always just tried to lose weight, and I never have made a decision to lose a certain amount and maintain the loss. The reason I believe I have avoided such a firm commitment is that I don't think I can really lose so much weight and keep it off. Both of my parents were large-boned, heavy people and I think I am basically just a large person. I don't think I would be happy as a smaller person." I questioned, "Were you ever a smaller person?" "Oh yes," replied Mr. Ray. "I was never heavy as a child. I didn't really start to get heavy until high school. I really wanted to play football, but I wasn't big enough or strong enough, so I worked really hard exercising, lifting weights, and eating as much as I could to build myself up for the football tryouts. I gained about thirty pounds over that summer, and I made the team. As long as I was playing football I maintained my weight at about 160 pounds, but after football season I put on more weight and I guess I have just been adding weight ever since." I said, "The fact that you were a smaller person and not a heavy, big-boned person as a child and early teenager strongly goes against your idea that your obesity is genetic from your parents." "I guess that's true," said Mr. Ray. "But then why am I so fat?" "Perhaps it is because you eat a great deal more than your body needs to maintain itself, and the excess goes to fat," I said. "But I really don't eat very much," mourned Mr. Ray. "My wife fixes me a very rigid diet of low fats and low cholesterol and only about one thousand calories a day. I can't understand, if it's not because I am just basically a large person why I don't lose weight." I questioned, "What else do you eat, other than what your wife fixes for you?" "I really don't eat anything else," responded Mr. Ray. "I sample a little bit from the delicatessen section of my grocery store to make sure all of the food is all right, but other than that I eat like a bird." "How frequently do you perform this quality control in the delicatessen?" I asked. "Well, you know how delicate and unstable many of those rich foods are, so I would say I probably check them every couple of hours," said Mr. Ray. "It sounds like you are gaining and maintaining your obesity through your quality control efforts," I replied. "Do you really think those few little spoonfuls could make the difference?" said Mr. Ray. "Unless you have some other place where your are getting the extra two or three thousand calories to maintain yourself, it looks like those few little spoonfuls are the answer," I explained. "That's amazing," said Mr. Ray. "I never would have thought that little bit could make such a difference. I'll tell you what I will do; I will stop testing the food for a week and see if I lose any weight. If the sampling is the problem, then my weight should drop."

Mr. Ray returned to the office a week later, eight pounds lighter. He reported that he felt as though he had been starving to death all week, but he had been able to restrain himself from nibbling, even though the temptation was enormous. I pointed out that it appeared the culprit was the food sampling. Mr. Ray had demonstrated that he was capable of losing weight and that he had no legitimate excuses for being so overweight. Therefore, if he chose to lose weight and be a smaller person, he was capable and knew how to do it. On the other hand, if he chose to remain obese that was certainly his right. Mr. Ray insisted that he wanted to lose weight and keep it off. We continued to work together over the next two years on a monthly basis. Mr. Ray lost 180 pounds and has maintained the loss to this day. He closed the delicatessen portion of his grocery store, as he realized it had never been profitable but served as his private gourmet feasting ground. Once he made a total body decision to change himself and he knew that he was capable of change, the daily process of losing the weight, as well as the maintenance, was fairly easy.

Mr. Ray is typical of many people who think they want to change but have strongly held beliefs which prevent them from confronting themselves and making the change. You have to work very hard at undermining any assumptions you have about your incapability of changing. Contrast and compare what you do when you are successful with what you are doing in the problem area. You will quickly see that you are consistently letting yourself off the hook in the problem area, but are using a very different communication to yourself where you are successful. There, you are strong and firm with yourself and do not allow any ideas, feelings, or intrusions to interrupt your success.

Changing

Changing is possibly the most difficult of all behaviors. We are all bound in a system which encourages the status quo. Inertia is a problem for nearly every human being. We work hard every day to maintain basically the same patterns of behavior of the day before. Habits become so ingrained that they are often performed routinely and ritualistically. The most common example is the morning ritual. Most of us do exactly the same thing every working morning and have trouble changing it on the weekends. We wake up at essentially the same time each day, clean our bodies, drink our coffee, dress for work, get in our cars, and travel the same route to work. There is very little deviation from the pattern. Because we can perform these rituals with very little thought and energy, they are useful and efficient. The problems arise when the old patterns are no longer appropriate but the rituals continue. For example, on vacation we may want to relax but our mind and body are programmed to keep on working. It often takes several days to make the transition to calm down, and in fact many people avoid vacations because they do not know how to stop themselves.

Thus, to maintain the status quo requires little energy and almost no conscious effort, but changing takes conscious effort and energy. Maintaining is fairly secure, predictable, and dull. Change is insecure, unpredictable, and exciting. Each of us must choose the balance between maintaining ourselves in old patterns of behavior and consciously choosing to upset those patterns by changing. People often complain of boredom and lack of excitement. Such people represent "the living dead." They have become so ingrained in patterns of behavior that there is nothing new and exciting in their lives. They insulate themselves from change by reinforcing the old patterns every day, but still they complain about it.

Most commonly the "living dead" are hard-working, well-meaning people who go through life in a daze. They may have been working at the same job for most of their lives and usually dislike the work but believe there is no alternative. They look forward to retirement. Each day represents another burden of boring, hated work, and is faced with gloom and sadness. They often develop physical diseases to avoid the routine. They look forward to weekends and vacations but have usually established similar dull patterns for their leisure time. A common example of static weekend activity is the obligation to mow the lawn every Saturday, wash the car, watch television Saturday evening, go to church Sunday morning, either sleep or visit relatives Sunday afternoon, then early to bed Sunday evening in preparation for Monday's labor. This pattern, which persists for years with minor modifications, is often viewed as essential to maintaining one's life. After all, the lawn must be mowed, and cars must be washed, and we have always gone to church on Sunday—it is the right thing to do. These people frequently complain about their lifestyle but they rarely do anything to change it. They view life as preplanned and view themselves as puppets acting out the plan. They do not take conscious responsibility either for their lives or for each of their behaviors. The concept of significant change is an unacceptable foreign issue to the "living dead." Recent advances in holistic medicine have opened many areas for responsible self-control and prevention of disease but these people see themselves as only passive participants in the disease process. This view is very similar to their view of life in general.

If you identify yourself as a card-carrying member of the "living dead" and wish to get out of that category, then you can. The first and perhaps most important step is to recognize that you have the problem and that you wish to make change. The vast majority of "living dead" do not know there is any other possibility. They are resistant to even hearing about possibilities for change; people who talk about taking charge of yourself are dismissed as fanatics or crazies. If you are willing to consider that you are not 100 percent happy with your life and if you wish to consciously take control and change some things, then you have accomplished the first step in changing.

The second step in making a change in yourself is to zero in on one really important aspect of your behavior that you are going to change. This behavior must be more important than anything else in your life and must be given your complete conscious attention. Stop worrying about all your other behaviors and feelings and focus on the big one you are going to change. This process of elimination of worries is hard for many people but it is critical. If you maintain fifty problems in your life and you go about trying to change everything, you will meet with frustration and failure. Many people protect themselves from change by setting up so many seemingly important things to change that they always feel overwhelmed and never can get themselves together enough to do anything. They reinforce their "living dead" status by their beliefs and behavior. Such comments as "I wouldn't know where to begin," or "Oh, I have so many problems, I could never work on just one at a time," are defenses against focusing and creating the possibility for change. This is not to say that there may not be several important areas of your life where you wish to make change. However, to be successful at consciously changing your behavior, you must work on only one area at a time. The others will wait until you get around to them. For instance, if you are fifty pounds overweight, a chain smoker, terrified to drive the car, and having major marital problems, you must choose one thing to change first and then move onto the others. Sometimes the choice of which is most important is purely arbitrary, but it must be done to be successful.

Once you have chosen the one behavior which you are going to change, the next step is to analyze your thoughts, rationalizations, and excuses for not changing. It is critical that you elicit all the excuses you have ever used to help yourself stick in this behavior. Don't be shy or kind to yourself and let yourself avoid some of the old, perhaps embarrassing excuses. Get them all out and carefully analyze and prove or disprove each one. Remember that this is the most important step in the process, because unless the supporting thoughts are modified, the behavior has no chance of being changed. Behavior follows thought and persists as long as it is supported by thought. As you pull out all the excuses and thoughts you have used over the years to perpetuate the behavior, you will be surprised at how easy it is to undermine and erode these beliefs. By freeing yourself of these old supporting ideas, you free yourself for change. Without the erosion and destruction of the ideas, you will not be able to change, because these thoughts tell you that you are not capable of changing.

A simple method of helping yourself get to all your excuses is to pay careful attention to the things you say to yourself. We all have unique methods of communicating to ourselves to get ourselves to do what we want to do. Some of these communication devices were outlined in Chapter III. The simple example of using the word *can't* to express one's inability when inability is not present is heard numerous times each day. If you pay careful attention to the real words you are saying to yourself you will quickly see that you are maintaining yourself in old patterns through these communications. Examine your speech. Don't assume that the words are not important or, worse, that they mean something other than their meaning. As you catch yourself using excuse words and words that maintain old patterns, stop yourself and ask, "Is that really true, or am I just saying that out of habit?" As you stop yourself and clear up the self-communication, you will find that eventually your communications to yourself and to others will take on a new accuracy. The process of clearing up your communications not only will help you understand and change yourself but will help you to be appreciated and respected by others. People who speak clearly and precisely are listened to much more than people who ramble on sloppily.

The next step in changing is to give yourself credit for what you do right and how you do it. In this step you examine your words, body posture, techniques and tone of voice used when you are successful. You will find that the essence of a successful communication is *meaningfulness*. Everyone who hears the communication knows that you mean it. In most cases of self-communication, no one else hears the words, but others witness the resultant behavior. Successful communications are often short and to the point. "I am leaving now." "I quit." "Stop." These messages are really clear. The other aspect of successful communication is its *importance*. When we speak clearly to ourselves or someone else, it is usually because what we are saying is really important. If you look at the successful behaviors in your life, you will see that where you are successful you have a strong belief that the issue is vital. You do not fool around with these behaviors but rather you take them seriously and do them right. A clear example is found in parent-child interactions when the child's life is endangered. Parents use absolutely clear communications in both words and behaviors to protect the child and teach the child to avoid such behavior in the future. No assumptions are made. Everything is spelled out and made crystal clear. The feeling behind successful communications is powerful commitment. This is the way it is going to be and there is no other possibility. It is this kind of self-communication that is often the basis for so-called miracle cures and survival in the face of extreme adversity. In these cases people make up their minds that they are going to be successful and they allow nothing else.

The last step is to know that you are capable of changing what you want to change, and to make it happen. Most people change only when they absolutely must, when all of the excuses, rationalizations, and alternatives have run out. The greatest opportunity for change is in crises. A crisis affords you a chance to do things differently because obviously the way you have been doing this isn't working very well. The Chinese character for crisis is the same as for opportunity, which demonstrates the ancient wisdom of understanding the opportunity in any crisis. When we are at the end of our rope, then we are willing to look at another way to go. Most of us, if we have any rope left at all, continue to hang on and avoid change. When there is no other choice but to go under or change, then we will examine the possibilities for change. Try to avoid the pain and sorrow of crises by consciously choosing to change before you get to the crisis. This means you must take conscious control of your own life, knowing that you are capable of changing yourself and putting forth the effort to do it. It means taking risks and venturing into unpredictable areas. Most of all it means being fully alive and conscious of what you are saying to yourself and what you are doing, and taking full responsibility for all success and failure . When you live your life fully, there is no failure because even if projects and new ventures do not work out, at least you had the fulfilling experience of putting yourself into it 100 percent to make it happen. For most people the greatest success and most fulfilling experience comes in the process of making things happen, rather than in the end product. A classic example of this phenomenon is the dating and courting that lead toward marriage. Most people recall that the process of the chase was exciting, fun, and greatly rewarding, whereas the end product of marriage is often viewed as dull, secure, and lifeless. Of course marriage doesn't have to be that way, but for many it is. The next step these people usually take is to start the courting process over with a new mate. Interestingly, in nearly dead marriages the same courtship process can be done with equally great rewards. However, many married couples don't think to start the courtship over because of all the assumptions and habit patterns they have built between them. They view the marriage as dead and give up. Remember, what you think is what you get.

Chapter 6

Making the Decision

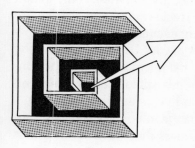

There is no such thing as a free lunch. Everything in life has a price and we do not have a choice about whether we wish to pay or not. We always pay the price. There is a high price for choosing to live among the "living dead." The price is fun, excitement, adventure, change, risk, and a feeling of really being alive. Are you willing to pay this price to maintain yourself the way you are? On the other hand, the price of living fully alive is security, stability, dullness, predictability, and status quo. We love our security and stability so much that we frequently sacrifice much of our life pursuing them, only to find that they actually do not exist. Real security and stability are internal, not external. We cannot ever achieve external stability in our world because it can always be taken from us by other people or by natural disasters. Internal security is personal and can never be taken away. It is self-love and respect and knowing your own self-worth and value as a human being.

The decision to make change in yourself is a very serious matter. Nobody changes unless they have to, or unless they become very aware of their life and make the conscious decision to change. Most of us live with the status quo and make minor adjustments in our lives to accommodate minimal change. It is truly infrequent that people set out consciously to change themselves significantly if they do not have to. It is the aim of this book to encourage and provide the tools for conscious change even though you can go on living without changing. The purposes of changing are to add a new dimension to your life, to venture into an area where you have never gone before, and to provide yourself with the opportunities to reach your highest potential in this lifetime. The status quo provides no challenge for your potential, but maintains you at a survival level. You may wish just to continue to survive from one day to the next, but the opportunity for changing is here if you wish to take it.

Real decision and 100 percent total body commitment are required to make conscious change. The image of 100 percent total body commitment comes from my experience working with fat people. It is not until every cell of the body is committed to losing weight and maintaining the loss that significant weight loss occurs. As you will remember in the case of the obese grocer, no real change took place until he made the total body decision to lose the weight and be a different person.

Accustomed to our habit patterns, we avoid anxiety over our negative aspects by denying that there is any problem or by believing that there is nothing we can do to change. Making a significant change in your behavior makes you a different person. You will not be the same and people will not treat you the same if you make a change in yourself. Thus you risk giving up all the predictables. You will be keenly aware that others are treating you differently and you will recognize subtle changes in the way you think about yourself. You have probably noticed that when you make even a very small change, such as a new hair style, different hair color, beard, or moustache, people react to you differently. Imagine how much greater the reaction if you make a major dramatic change in yourself.

Your internal recognition of such a change is much slower than the outside world's recognition of it. People who change their body image by losing weight, doing body-building exercise, or undergoing surgery often take several years before they really feel themselves differently. It appears that the longer you have been in the old habit pattern, the longer it takes to see and feel yourself differently. A common example is the obese person who loses a significant amount of weight. While the rest of the world sees him as thin and shapely, he often continues to view himself as obese despite all external evidence. The mind is slow to change its perception of oneself after years of programming and reinforcement. This is not to discourage you from making changes and enjoying them in yourself but is meant as reassurance for the time when you make a change but don't feel it right away. Give yourself time and pay attention to the feedback from your friends. Our self-view is determined from the input we receive from the outside world combined with the way we perceive ourselves.

When you make a decision to change yourself, you must make a *commitment to do whatever you have to do to make the change.* If you find yourself saying, "Now, wait a minute, it depends on what I have to do and how hard it is," then forget it. Unless you are willing to go all the way and put everything you've got into making the change, your chances of success are small. On the other hand, if you feel really strongly about making change and have gone through the steps outlined in the previous chapters, and if you know that you are capable of making the change, then you stand a good chance of success.

The decision and commitment are tied up with your energy to change. Change requires energy. It usually doesn't take any more energy to change than you have been expending maintaining yourself in the old patterns, but initially it feels like it is taking more energy. This feeling is the mind and body defense against making change. There is a strong feeling of inertia. You must use the power of your mind, as expressed through commitment and decision, to keep yourself moving toward change. It is almost never a question of capability to change, but rather a question of strength of commitment to change that makes the difference. This phenomenon is seen in people who develop serious heart disease or lung cancer and are told they must stop smoking. These people stop not because they want to, but because they make a serious decision to live longer. Obviously, the capability to stop smoking was always present but the motivation was never strong enough. When you consciously choose to change a behavior, if there is nobody pushing you to do it and your life is not threatened, you must create the same internal motivation to get the same results. As children we are very lucky because parents make decisions for us and force us to change behaviors that are negative or self-destructive. When we become adults there is no one outside ourselves who can apply this pressure to make change. We must use our minds and motivate ourselves out of conscious desire to change, then work up our energy and commitment to make it happen.

The following case demonstrates the idea of commitment, decision, and energy.

Frank was a 32-year-old successful lawyer, married to a nurse, father of three beautiful young children. Three years prior to my meeting him, Frank had made a major decision and had lost forty pounds which he had been carrying around as excessive weight since he was a small child. This significant weight loss represented the first major personal change in Frank's life and he was pleased with his ability to make a decision and follow it through. At the time of our meeting, Frank was in the hospital suffering from severe infectious hepatitis, a life-threatening disease and was seriously depressed. He had been hospitalized for three weeks and was growing progressively worse each day. His doctors gave him less than

40 percent chance for survival and there was no treatment available for his condition. Frank's wife was involved in self-awareness, self-hypnosis, and laying on of hands and believed that he could be helped by using his internal resources; however, her attempts to motivate him toward overcoming his illness were unsuccessful. Frank was playing the classic passive dependent patient role and taking no responsibility for his illness or his treatment. He was cooperative with the nurses and doctors, but became progressively more ill each day.

I confronted Frank regarding his will to live and discovered that he was ambivalent regarding continuing his life. He had been very successful in doing most of the things he had set out to do and felt satisfied with his life. Through his wife he had been working at becoming more aware of himself and felt satisfaction in his life. He had no fear of dying, as he looked forward to the transition of death.

Interestingly, Frank had become very involved with a number of clients involved in life-threatening and dying circumstances. He was fascinated by a few of them who had used mind control techniques to prolong life and in several cases cured themselves of so-called incurable diseases; he was also perplexed that other clients who appeared to use the same techniques were unsuccessful. Frank was very cooperative with me and excited that I was also interested in these same kinds of phenomena and had worked with numerous patients to help them help themselves to overcome disease.

In the process of working with Frank, I taught him the techniques of deep relaxation and meditation and of getting in touch with his inner self. Frank was highly motivated and worked hard relaxing himself and communicating with his inner self. On the second day of deep meditation, Frank reported that his inner voice had told him that the reason he was sick with this untreatable disease was to prove to himself and to others that he was capable of overcoming it. His excitement upon getting this insight was outstanding. He called me in the middle of the night and said he had to learn the techniques for self-healing immediately. I got out of bed and went to Frank's bedside and spent the rest of the night teaching him to use the natural power of his mind. Frank was 100 percent committed to overcoming his disease and had no doubts about his ability to succeed. He began to improve immediately and turned his hospital course around. Two weeks later Frank was discharged from the hospital, to the amazement of his doctors, who labeled him a "miracle cure." Three weeks after his discharge, Frank and his family took a long-planned vacation to Europe against his doctors' advice. He knew that he was completely cured and saw no reason to cancel the trip. Frank had no further illness and no further problems from the illness.

The experience of this illness changed Frank's life. He stopped working twelve to fourteen hours a day six days a week and cut back to about eight hours a day four days a week. He involved himself in training programs to achieve higher states of awareness and began sharing his experience and new-found knowledge with his friends, colleagues, and most recently teaching classes in self-control. In looking back, Frank explains his illness as the greatest opportunity of his life. He recognized that he was at the crossroads between life and death and in his case the decision was completely his. He took control of himself, made the decision to live, and committed himself to change. The follow-up on Frank, now several years later, shows him to be happier than ever before in his life. Not only has he had no recurrence of the original illness but he has not suffered any other diseases of any kind since his dramatic recovery. He is living his life fully for the first time and is joyous about the opportunity. Frank and his family now look for challenges, risks, and opportunities to live fully and are an exciting example to anyone who meets them.

The story of Frank demonstrates total body commitment. He made the conscious decision to change himself and demonstrated that decision through his actions. You must be willing to do whatever you have to do to make the change. You must be willing to do the same thing with your body that you are saying with your mouth. Many people give lip service to the idea of making change but few of them follow through and give the same message with their bodies. When we only agree to make change or just think about making change, nothing significant happens. When we put our whole bodies in synchronization with our thoughts, the change takes place.

You must erase doubt and replace it with knowledge that you are capable and will make the change. The occasional stories of 100-pound mothers lifting a car off their children after an accident portrays the power of knowing you can do it. In those cases, the mothers did not stop and question "I wonder if I can lift that car off the child." Instead they saw the crisis and responded almost instinctively, protecting their young, never questioning whether or not they were capable of doing it. It is this kind of 100 percent total body commitment that works to make change. Other names for this experience are faith, trust, and will. We have all heard of people who lost the will to live. In almost all cases, if a person does not have that driving force of will to live, then he or she succumbs. On the other hand, there have been numerous examples through history of people who had extraordinarily strong wills to live and who experienced all kinds of life-threatening problems but always overcame them. Many of the lessons in the Bible teach us of the capacity and power of the mind when one has faith. Examine your commitment, decision, faith, and will to do whatever you have to do to change; then set about doing whatever you must.

Chapter 7

How to Help Yourself Change

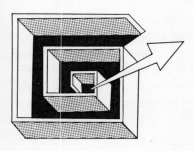

We live in a stressful world. There is no way to avoid stressful experiences. Many people try to run away from stress by changing jobs, moving to rural areas, taking pills, or trying other methods which do not work. It seems that no matter what the occupation or life circumstances of a person, the complaints always center around some kind of stress and a feeling of inability to cope. Background and socioeconomic status make no difference in whether one experiences the stress of life. Most people have a fantasy that if they were wealthy or if they lived somewhere else or if they had a different occupation or boss, then the stress would be less. It doesn't work that way.

The experience of stress begins in very early life. Even in the womb we experience frustration and discomfort and move around trying to change our experience. Once we are born into the world we experience the stresses of hunger, pain, cold, heat, light, and so forth, all of which we must handle. In our childhood we confront stressors at every turn and cope with them as best we can given the minimal tools at our disposal. Among the most common coping devices children use are the development of symptoms. Headaches, stomach aches, fears, and phobias are frequently seen in children who do not have other tools to cope with their stress. In addition, many of the childhood illnesses are made worse by the associated stresses. Adults do an excellent job of teaching their children to respond to stress with anxiety. The most common universal complaints revolve around tension, anxiety, and their concomitant somatic manifestations. In the United States the most frequently prescribed drugs are the anti-anxiety medications. Recent polls have shown that more than one-half of the population uses the relaxing effect of marijuana to deal with tension and anxiety. Of course, we are all familiar with the heavy use of alcohol to deal with stress. All of this evidence about use of external chemical methods to deal with tension supports the notion that we are not trained to cope with everyday stress.

Learning to manage the stresses in your daily life is much easier than you might think. Unfortunately, until recently there has been no emphasis on learning how to handle stress internally. It has been assumed that somehow everybody should just know how to cope with stress; the concept of learning specific techniques for relaxing has been ignored. In the past few years the disastrous effects of stress, tension, and anxiety have been recognized internationally and massive efforts are being made to help people handle their stresses more effectively. Many industries now have stress management programs for their employees as they have recognized the mortality and morbidity from stress. Medical and paramedical personnel have developed a new field called Holistic Medicine, whose philosophy integrates mind, body, and spirit. Relaxation and stress reduction are fundamental to integrating the total self. A very important advance in self-control and relaxation is biofeedback. Through the use of simple electronic monitors, a person is actually able to see and hear himself relaxing various muscle groups of the body. The biofeedback equipment does not relax people, but it provides proof that people are capable of making changes in their tension levels. For many people who have little faith in their innate internal abilities, this proof is very powerful. The biofeedback data have also legitimized the area of stress control and raised it to a more scientific measurable level. We now know that through training we are able to control literally every function of our bodies.

In this section, some very simple proven methods of gaining greater self-control will be explained. A foundation of deep relaxation is exceedingly helpful for making any significant change in one's life. You may already have experienced some type of relaxation or meditation program. If you have a set of techniques which works well to keep yourself in a high-functioning relaxed state, then you probably do not need the information in this chapter. Use your particular techniques to get yourself into the relaxed state and allow yourself to use the material from the earlier chapters to make the changes you desire. When you are at peace with yourself and relaxed, the process of making change is much more effective and much easier. Many people have found that in the relaxed state they are more effective in clarifying what is really important for them to change and in eliciting and eroding their belief systems. In the tense, stressful state you are functioning at low-level efficiency and have much less chance for success. The following simple techniques and tools will help to ensure your success in changing yourself.

The process of relaxation, meditation, or self-hypnosis all have essentially the same end result. When the mind is used to relax the muscles of the body, a condition of self-control is achieved which in turn relaxes and reassures the mind. The result is a state of peacefulness in which the mind and body are totally relaxed and in the highest state of health. It is in this state—sometimes called the alpha state, trance, or meditative state—that we are able to get in touch with our deep inner selves and experience our highest potential. For many people this wonderful relaxed calm state is achieved through disciplined meditation but for many others the experience comes through physical activity such as working in the garden, jogging, sailing, or floating down river on a rubber raft. There is no right way to relax yourself. There are thousands of ways which can be used and each of us must find what works best for us. It is important to accept that whatever way you choose to calm yourself is right for you. Be sure that you are really achieving a deep sense of peace and calm in your method. If you find that you never feel really totally relaxed and at peace, that thoughts keep running through your head and that you remain agitated, then perhaps some of the techniques described here will be helpful. Again, don't make judgments about whether you are doing it right or wrong. You will know when you have achieved the calm, peaceful state.

The majority of people find it difficult to just sit down in a comfortable position in silence and relax themselves. We are so accustomed to doing something that it is very hard to sit quietly, clear our minds, and relax our bodies. A simple aid to help you relax and gain greater self-control is relaxing music. Probably the most relaxing sounds ever recorded are the Golden Voyage series, Volumes I, II, and III (particularly Volume I). These are available from Awakening Productions (4132 Tuller Avenue, Culver City, California 90230). Robert Bearns and Ron Dexter have combined the world's most relaxing natural sounds with simple, soothing melodies for a combination of sounds that can relax almost anyone. Many have found that their biggest problem while listening to these sounds is keeping awake. Sit in a comfortable chair with arms and legs unfolded and your head supported by a pillow or the back of the chair and just listen to the sounds. Other pieces of music are also very soothing but to be really effective the sounds should not be familiar tunes which bring thoughts to your mind. The natural sounds of waterfalls, streams, birds, and the like tend to create mental images of peaceful relaxation, which is the first step in greater self-control and ultimate change.

Begin your training by finding a time in your day when you can isolate yourself and have peace and quiet. Plan to spend at least fifteen to twenty minutes uninterrupted, once or twice a day. If you live in a noisy, busy environment and cannot arrange for a quiet place and time, then look outside your home, perhaps to your car, office, or other place where you can find a quiet, uninterrupted space. Once you have trained yourself to relax, you will find it takes only a few seconds to achieve the depth and calm you need.

It is also important to set aside a time when you have energy and good concentration ability. Remember that this exercise is your gift to yourself and should be respected and treated with a high priority. Putting off your relaxation training until the end of the day, just before bed, is putting yourself at the bottom of the priority list. Most people who do this fall asleep in the middle of the training and do not really benefit themselves. Find a time when you are fresh, alive, and full of energy to put into yourself.

Once you have established a time and place for your relaxation self-control training, the next step is either to listen to the music or to sit in silence, allowing yourself to go deeper and deeper into yourself. The most frequent problem is the occurrence of stray thoughts which come to mind while you are trying to calm yourself. When these thoughts come, just allow them to pass by like scenery passing as you drive along a road. Do not stop and pay attention to these ideas but let them go by. If the thoughts are important for you to remember, make a mental note and you will remember when you are finished relaxing. It is important not to judge yourself as doing a good or bad job. Remember there is no right or wrong way of relaxing and controlling yourself. There is only your way of doing it for you, that will become clear as you try these different approaches.

Another frequently used approach to calming yourself is to concentrate on a particular object or imaginary spot. For others the use of a verbal sound, like a mantra, is helpful in calming and relaxing the mind and body. Any sound which is pleasing to you is appropriate. You can use a humming sound or the traditional "Om" sound. Others concentrate on their breathing by focusing all their concentration on the experience of the air passing across the end of the nose with the in and out breath. Again there is no right or proper way. Try different methods and find which one works to calm you.

For those who are sedentary in their usual daytime jobs, a physically active relaxation is often preferable. Some kind of personal exercise such as jogging, swimming, bike riding, or walking may serve to cleanse your mind and relax your body. As you go about the physical activity, pay attention to the fact that your body and mind are becoming more and more relaxed, and begin to condition your mind and body to the experience of being relaxed.

Being relaxed is a learned and conditioned phenomenon. It does not happen by accident, and if it is inborn it is quickly conditioned out. Use whatever method works to relax yourself and teach your mind what it feels like to be relaxed. Eventually, you will be able to achieve the deeply relaxed state by just telling yourself to relax or conditioning yourself to a stimulus, like a deep breath, which gives you the deep relaxation instantly. What you are doing is training your muscles in how to relax. This kind of training is the same as that used in learning to ride a bicycle or attaining any other body skill. The muscles have to learn what to do so they can do it on command.

A technique which has been useful to many people is a

form of progressive muscle relaxation training. The muscles are relaxed, one group at a time, through a comparison of contraction and relaxation. This is an active process, requiring concentration on the act of contracting and relaxing the muscles, and therefore it serves as a focus of concentration for the mind. It has been found that when one is successful in relaxing the muscles of the body, the mind also relaxes, probably as a by-product of the concentration and focusing. The following procedure may be used as a guide for progressively relaxing your muscles.

Sit comfortably in a chair with your arms and legs uncrossed. Close your eyes and focus all of your attention on the muscles of your face. Contract all the muscles of your face by squinting your eyes, frowning your forehead, and gritting your teeth together as hard as you can. Hold this position for five seconds, then release it completely. Remain in the relaxed state for approximately fifty-five seconds, and then repeat the process. Do this same contraction and relaxation process for the other major muscle groups of the body. A simple plan to follow is, head, both arms and shoulders, chest and abdomen, and both legs. Many people begin by concentrating on smaller groups of muscles, such as one arm at a time; as you experience being more or less relaxed, you will determine whether you need to break it down more. If the short method doesn't do the trick after a few sessions, then expand the process and work with fewer muscles at a time. The purpose of this exercise is to teach your brain what it feels like to have your muscles relaxed.

Most people have trouble doing these exercises silently. You might use a tape recorder. Tape yourself instructing yourself in the relaxation technique, and when you do the exercise you can play the tape and have yourself as your guide and teacher. Again, these crutches are usually necessary only in the early stages of learning to relax yourself. Here is a suggested patter for your tape.

"Sit comfortably in your chair and concentrate on the muscles of your face. Tighten all the muscles of your face now. Feel the tension and the tightness, feel the muscles pull, feel the hardness as the muscles tighten and contract; experience the tension; now relax. Just relax, letting all the tension go, focusing on these muscles as they just relax completely, noticing what it feels like as the muscles become more and more relaxed, focusing all your attention on the feelings associated with relaxation flowing into these muscles; just enjoying the pleasant feelings of relaxation, as the muscles go on relaxing more and more deeply, more and more completely. There's nothing for you to do but focus your attention on the very pleasant feelings of relaxation flowing into this area. Just noticing what it's like as the muscles become more and more deeply relaxed; just enjoying the feelings in the muscles as they loosen up, smooth out, unwind, and relax more and more deeply. Just experiencing the sensations of deep, complete relaxation flowing into these muscles; more and more deeply and completely relaxed. Just letting them go, thinking about nothing but the very pleasant feelings of relaxation. Just let those muscles go and notice how they feel now as compared to before. Notice how those muscles feel when so completely relaxed. Pay attention only to the sensations of relaxation as the relaxation process takes place. Calm, peaceful, and relaxed."

If you want more information about this technique of Progressive Relaxation Training, you may consult the book

Progressive Relaxation Training by Douglas Bernstein and Thomas Borhover (Research Press, 1973).

Another useful technique for getting yourself more relaxed is a breathing exercise in which you use breath control and talk to yourself. This approach is valuable because it not only teaches self-control and relaxation but plants important positive information about yourself in your mind. The repetitions of this technique result in a greater sense of self-esteem and an increased awareness of one's ability to reach his or her highest potential. In this approach you sit comfortably, take a long, slow, deep breath, and hold it for approximately thirty seconds. Then, as you slowly release the breath, say to yourself, "My arms and legs are heavy and warm." Take another long, slow, deep breath and hold it; then, as you slowly release it, say, "My forehead is warm." Then take another deep breath, hold it, and while slowly releasing it say to yourself, "My abdomen is warm and heavy." Take one more long, slow, deep breath, hold it, then on slowly releasing it say, "I feel calm and at peace." Then in this relaxed state talk to yourself about how heavy your body feels and how warm it feels as the muscles relax and the blood flows into the muscles. Reinforce yourself about what a good job you are doing relaxing yourself and how good it feels to be in a healthy state of relaxation.

Many people favor an approach which combines both the muscle relaxation and breathing technique. Begin by sitting comfortably with your body completely supported by the chair and your head supported by a pillow or the chair. Roll your eyes up into your forehead as far as you can and hold them there while at the same time you slowly close your eyelids. (This is not an easy exercise at first, but you will quickly pick it up with practice.) When your eyes are closed, take a long, slow, deep breath, and as you release it slowly say to yourself, "Calm, *C A L M.*" Repeat this breathing and spelling for five long, slow inhales and exhales. Allow your eyes to be at rest with your eyelids closed. Next, concentrate on your muscles, one group at a time. Tighten the muscles of your arms and legs by pointing your toes toward your nose and at the same time making fists and contracting your biceps and triceps. Then relax all these muscles of your arms and legs for about one minute. Next tighten the muscles of your chest and abdomen by pulling in a deep breath, holding it, and at the same time pulling in your stomach as far as you can. Hold this position for about five seconds and release it, relaxing and concentrating on the feeling of relaxation compared to tension for about one minute. Last, concentrate on the muscles of your face and neck and tighten those muscles by pulling your chin down on your chest while at the same time pulling it back toward your shoulders and also squinting up your face. Then relax, and enjoy the experience of the muscles smoothing out and being at peace. In the next step, deepen the relaxation with five long, slow, deep breaths, breathing in deeper and deeper relaxation and expelling any tension or tightness that may be remaining in your body. To bring yourself back into the reality of your space, clench both of your fists, take three deep, energizing breaths, and experience yourself breathing in energy, awakeness, and aliveness. On the third breath open your eyes and your fists and feel good.

Visualization and Imagery

Once you have mastered the art of relaxing and calming yourself, you can move into the exciting area of imagery and visualization. In the past few years neuroscientists have learned a great deal about the functioning of the brain. One of the most interesting phenomena discovered is the enormous power of the brain to change bodily functions when images or pictures are created in the mind. The scientists have discovered that the right half of the brain is concerned primarily with images, pictures, fantasies, and intuition, while the left half of the brain is concerned primarily with thinking and logical processes. Up until recently most of the work in helping people to change has been done using thoughts and logical verbal stimuli. Now we know that an even greater power exists in our right brain: if we can learn to develop images of what we want, the body in turn responds by changing things to make the images real. A fascinating and unique property of the mind is its inability to differentiate between what is real and what is imagined. The mind cannot tell the difference between what you actually see and what you see with your eyes closed. A demonstration of this fact is the power of dreams. Most of us have had dreams that were so real that they startled us or woke us up. Many people have such realistic dreams that it takes them several minutes after awakening to figure out whether it was a dream or the real thing. A frequent example in children is the dream of having to go to the bathroom, then dreaming that they get out of bed, go to the bathroom, and are using the toilet, only to wake up and find that they have just wet the bed. Dreams are right-brain experiences and are real to the dreamer.

An interesting physiologic experience has been documented to demonstrate the power of the mind to change bodily functions. It has been known that waterfalls are very relaxing places for people. However, no one ever knew why they were so relaxing. Recently neurobiologists have discovered that waterfalls create a very high concentration of negatively charged ions in the air around them. The same high concentration of negatively charged ions occurs after a thunderstorm. It has been learned that the brain and body respond to these negative ions by relaxing, calming down, and mellowing out. What is so fascinating is that exactly the same result can be achieved by listening to the sound of a waterfall or imagining yourself next to a waterfall or stream. The mind experiences the sound or the image as the real thing and sets the brain and nervous system into action, with relaxation the result. The wonderful thing about this information is that it means we can make all sorts of things happen to ourselves by just imagining them. An example from the area of hypnosis may serve to clarify the power and value of this information.

Mrs. Jacks is a 47-year-old woman with severe rheumatoid arthritis. She came to me for help in controlling her pain, which was primarily in her knees, hands, and neck. I taught her the techniques of deep relaxation and then hypnotized her and presented the image that both of her hands were in buckets of ice and becoming very cold and numb. Once she had complete numbness in her hands, I instructed her to place her hands on any area of her body where there was pain and to allow the numbness and cold to go into the painful area. Mrs. Jacks first relieved the pain in her knees and then removed the pain in her neck. When she came out of the light trance, she had no pain at all. She described a vivid image of her hands in the buckets of ice and clearly saw the numbness and pain-free feelings passing from her hands into her knees and neck. Mrs. Jacks was taught to use these same techniques at home and was able to reduce her need for pain medicine dramatically.

Recent work using imagery for every conceivable problem has demonstrated that there does not appear to be any limit to the power of the images to change bodily functions.

Among the most publicized uses of this approach is the work of Carl and Stephanie Simonton at the Cancer Counseling and Research Center in Fort Worth, Texas. The Simmontons have been using relaxation and imagery in the treatment of cancer, with remarkable results. They help cancer patients overcome the disease using visual images of the body's natural defense, the immune system, to combat and destroy the tumor. Their technique and results are presented in their book *Getting Well Again* (Tarcher Press, 1979). Many others, including the author, have had personal experience using imagery to combat cancer and other acute and chronic diseases, with truly outstanding success. These are not miracle cures. It takes very hard work and discipline to practice and use imagery on a regular basis. It also takes the absolute faith and belief that you will be successful. Without the strength of your convictions, the images will not form clearly and thoughts and distractions will hinder success. If you have the will to change and are 100 percent committed to changing, you will be successful. As you practice and create in your mind the images of what you want to happen, the body gets the message to make that condition happen. Then the complex machinery of the biochemical and nervous system is set into motion and changes begin to occur through the natural physiologic processes.

Chapter 8

Applying the Method

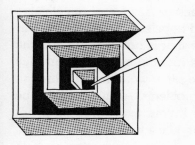

In the preceding chapters the techniques of changing yourself have been presented and explained. This chapter describes the most common kinds of problems which people have and shows how these techniques can be used to overcome these problems. The problems are broken down into three categories: *Escapes, Performance Problems,* and *Bad Habits.* Nearly all of the behavior problems from which people suffer fit under one of these.

The case example cited is probably not exactly like your problem, but if you allow yourself a little flexibility, you can apply it to yourself quite easily. Beware of maintaining your feeling of helplessness and hopelessness by seeing your problem as so unique that one that is not exactly the same won't be relevant. People have more in common than they have different. We are all in the same world and go through pretty much the same kinds of problems. Allow yourself to be open enough to help yourself. If your exact problem is not cited in this book, see if you can place yourself in one of the three broad categories and apply the information to help yourself.

Category One—Escapes

Escapes are the tricks we play on ourselves to avoid dealing directly with our world. Of course, there really is no escape from this world but many people work very hard at avoiding confrontation with reality. When one is truly alive there is no need for escape, because every problem is viewed as a challenge for new growth. When problems are seen as opportunities to learn and grow, there is no negative feeling and no reason to try to escape.

The most common kind of escape is to change your state of consciousness to be less aware of your world. This is frequently done through alcohol, drugs, or medications. Another equally effective method is to change your body so that you are less able to interact with the world. This kind of escape is typified by obesity, extreme thinness, fragility, and sickliness. In the extreme cases, one can induce blindness or paralysis to avoid such interaction. These extreme states of denial and escape are known as *conversion reactions* and can result in a lifetime of misery for the individual and his or her family.

Another common escape is depression and physical illness. How often do you get a headache to avoid doing something you don't want to do? Most of us are much more comfortable with physical symptoms than we are with emotional symptoms. We frequently convert emotional feelings of depression, loneliness, sadness, and helplessness into physical symptoms. Our friends and family are more sympathetic to physical problems than to psychological problems.

Carefully evaluate yourself and see if you are escaping from really being alive. If you find that you are using some of the escape methods described here, then you can use the techniques from the preceding chapters and the case material to help yourself overcome the problems.

CASE 1—EXCESSIVE DRINKING

Harry was a 34-year-old aerospace worker who was married for a second time, with two children by his first wife and one by his current wife. He was active in his community and was liked and respected by everyone who knew him. Harry never believed he had a problem with alcohol until the night he fell asleep at the wheel driving home from an evening with friends and hit another car head on. He and four other people were hospitalized. Fortunately no one was killed, but two of the persons in the other car were seriously injured. Lying in the hospital, Harry realized he had a problem with alcohol.

It is not significant to argue whether Harry was an alcoholic or not; the point is that he used alcohol to escape. He had been following a heavy drinking pattern for about ten years. He usually started drinking wine at lunch, then had a couple of glasses of wine upon getting home from work. He commonly had two or three martinis before dinner. His total alcohol intake per day averaged about a liter of wine and fifteen ounces of hard liquor. Harry did not become drunk or obviously intoxicated, but he numbed himself and decreased his awareness of his world. No one would have ever thought that Harry had a drinking problem because most of the time he was no problem to anyone else. In fact, when Harry announced to his wife that he was an alcoholic, her first reaction was to say that it wasn't true, that he was just a social drinker. Fortunately Harry had thought a lot about himself, knew that he had a serious problem, and had made up his mind to change.

Harry called me and asked me to visit him in the hospital. He told me that he wanted to stop drinking and was willing to work as hard as necessary to be successful. I helped him to get through the withdrawal phase and supported him in his ability to avoid drinking. I demanded that Harry attend Alcoholics Anonymous meetings every night for two weeks then at least one meeting per week thereafter. Harry's wife was instructed to attend Al-Anon meetings for the families of alcoholics. Harry quickly made friends at A.A. and developed a strong support system from this group. Every day that he stayed away from alcohol, he found himself feeling better and more alive. His energy increased, his memory improved, and his relationship with his wife and children was better. Harry has been "dry" for one year and reports feeling like a new person, enjoying all of life each day with no escapes.

The case of Harry is similar to that of many people who drink excessively. They refuse to recognize that they are escaping from much of their lives. When they get into a crisis, they have an opportunity to see themselves more clearly and make a decision to change. Changing a long-standing drinking problem is hard work and requires a strong personal commitment plus a strong network of supporters. The Alcoholics Anonymous programs provide the best source of external support and are extremely helpful in overcoming this problem. Very few people are successful in changing a heavy drinking pattern on their own. Don't be afraid to ask for help from people who have been where you are. One of the rewards in A.A. is the reinforcement you get by helping others with the same problem.

CASE 2 —OBESITY

Mrs. Kay was a typical overweight middle-aged housewife who had tried every diet on the market, with no significant success. She nearly killed herself on the liquid protein diet and was hospitalized for a short period for heart irregularities. She had also had H.C.G. shots and had lost seventy pounds, but as usual had gained the weight back in a few months following the shots. When she came to me she stated she was desperate and willing to do anything. A friend of hers had worked with me using visual imagery for weight loss, with great success, and Mrs. Kay was convinced she too could be successful using that method.

I instructed Mrs. Kay that she was to eat anything she wanted and that she did not have to do any exercise. All she had to do was deeply relax herself and visually imagine herself exactly the size and shape she desired. She was given detailed instructions in this technique and was required to perform the imagery at least four times a day. Mrs. Kay was determined to be successful this time and practiced the relaxation and imagery up to ten times a day in the first week. She did not diet and was not careful about what she was eating. She reported a two-pound weight loss in the first week and felt disappointed.

I asked her to remove her scale from her home and avoid weighing herself at any time. I explained that the goal of the treatment was not her weight but rather achieving the figure she desired. She was further instructed in the techniques of seeing herself standing in front of a "magic mirror" which showed her in vivid detail exactly the size, shape, and proportion she desired. She was also informed that for the body to realize itself to her image, it would have to make significant biochemical changes and that the process was natural and slow. She was encouraged to develop the visualization as part of a daily routine and otherwise not be concerned about her weight or size. Appointments were scheduled at monthly intervals.

Mrs. Kay slowly and progressively began losing weight, and her body realined itself to a new figure. Unconsciously and effortlessly Mrs. Kay found herself avoiding fattening foods. At the same time she developed an interest in active exercises, beginning with walking and moving up to jogging and bike riding, eventually enrolling in a dance exercise class. When people commented on her new appearance after she had lost twenty to thirty pounds but was still obese, Mrs. Kay responded by saying, "I really am thin and beautiful, aren't I." Mrs. Kay developed a strong, powerful image of herself as a thin person, and no matter how the world saw her, to herself she was thin and shapely.

Ultimately Mrs. Kay lost eighty-five pounds, leveling off at a good weight for her body build. She was very pleased with herself and has never regained any excess weight. She continues to practice once a day seeing her perfect self and reports feeling better than ever before in her life.

The secret of Mrs. Kay's success was her belief in herself, her discipline in practicing the imagery, and her absolute commitment to change. Once she established the image in her mind of exactly the way she was to be, her body took over and did the rest. The reason I took away the scale was to protect Mrs. Kay from the reminder that she was not yet where she wanted to be. When the element of conflict between the image and reality keeps popping up, it makes the process less effective. After Mrs. Kay used the imagery for approximately a month, she clearly saw herself as a thin person and no matter what the mirror showed or people said, she was thin. It is this consistent and persistent message to the brain that changes the biochemistry and keeps it changed. The unconscious change of diet and exercise took place naturally in accordance with the image. It took Mrs. Kay approximately one year to fit her physical body into her imaginary body, but she will never have to worry about gaining weight again as long as she maintains her image.

CASE 3—SMOKING

Bill was a chronic three-pack-a-day smoker. He stated that he was fed up with smoking and all of its health and social problems, and had decided to quit. He called me because he believed hypnosis would help him to stop. Bill had been smoking for more than twenty years and had never quit. In the previous five years he had become much more conscious of his health; he was jogging and was eating only a vegetarian diet.

I inquired about any vivid adversive taste that Bill could

remember. He immediately responded with a clear visual memory of an expensive dinner party at which the only choice to eat was beef and kidney pie. Bill related he tried in every way to avoid eating the beef and kidney pie but there was no way out under the circumstances. He put a forkful of the pie in his mouth, began to chew it, and immediately felt sick to his stomach. He excused himself from the table and went to the bathroom, where he spit it out. He gave his hosts the excuse that he was recovering from a stomach flu and was not feeling up to par. The image of this experience left such a strong impression on Bill that even talking about it made him feel queasy.

The next step in the treatment was to put Bill in a deep state of relaxation. Once he was deeply relaxed, I had him experience himself smoking a cigarette, in his mind. As he experienced the smoke in his mouth, I suggested that the smoke tasted exactly like the beef and kidney pie. Bill was instructed that he could continue smoking as much as he desired and that he would have desires for cigarettes in the future. However, anytime he put cigarette smoke in his mouth he would experience the taste of the beef and kidney pie.

No further appointments were scheduled for Bill, and telephone follow-up revealed that he had not smoked any cigarettes during the two years following our one session. A very critical point in Bill's success was his high motivation to change. He had carefully examined his life and decided the most important change he wanted to make was to stop smoking. He had reviewed his ability to make major changes in his life and knew that he had been successful previously during three job changes and two moves across country. Bill knew he was capable and had made up his mind that he was going to stop smoking. The use of the deep relaxation and adversive imagery was merely a crutch to help him over the final hurdle in making the change. There was no magic in Bill's great success. He was determined and committed and made it happen for himself.

CASE 4 —I DEPRESSION

Don was a 45-year-old successful physician who had been chronically depressed off and on most of his life. He had spent three years in intensive psychoanalysis, with minimal change in his depression. Two years prior to seeing me, he and his wife had agreed to a divorce as they felt they both contributed to each other's depression. After the marital split Don had involved himself with several new relationships but was unable ever to feel very happy. He was obsessed about details, future plans, and money. He never felt really satisfied or complete. Since the marriage breakup Don had begun drinking quite heavily and was using stimulants and tranquilizers to try to help himself. He had tried anti-depressant medication on himself but felt it had no significant effect.

Don was a workaholic. He spent fourteen to sixteen hours a day in his practice and at the hospital. He said he felt best when he was working so hard that he had no time to think of anything else. His social life was limited to parties where he drank heavily and frequently passed out. He gained weight and was approximately forty pounds overweight and in bad physical condition. He did no exercise and took no time from his busy schedule for himself. He tried to relieve his depression by buying adult toys; he had accumulated three large boats, an airplane and two sports cars plus a luxury car. He saw his children every other weekend but did not enjoy them because when he was with them he felt anxious, and generally inadequate.

Don's early life history was not particularly traumatic. His father had strongly encouraged high achievement from the children, and his mother had been loving and warm. Don had worked to make money since age 7 and he had always believed that money was happiness. He had worked through his authority conflicts in his psychoanalysis but remained depressed. Don occassionally thought of suicide but had never consciously attempted to kill himself. He had fallen asleep at the wheel on several occasions and had several auto accidents. He had married early in his career, hoping that he would be happier with a wife. But to his dismay he found that no one outside himself could bring him happiness. He had tried several affairs, but again, was always left feeling down.

Don reached the point of desperation. Several of his colleagues and friends became concerned about him and encouraged him to see me. As usual, I asked if he was willing to sacrifice and do whatever he had to do to change himself. Don reluctantly agreed and the treatment began with Don signing a contract agreeing to give up his depression. The next step was to limit his diet to 1,000 calories per day until he lost the excess forty pounds. In addition Don was instructed to walk briskly twenty minutes three times a week, moving up to a slow jog as quickly as possible. At this point Don believed that he hated exercise and didn't have the twenty minutes to give to something he didn't want to do. He was offered the choice of doing as he was told or finding another therapist. He agreed to follow the prescribed plan.

On the second visit, approximately one week later, Don reported feeling a little better but not happy yet. I suggested that he wasn't doing enough for himself as yet and I prescribed a meditation exercise of listening to the Golden Voyage tape three times a day while sitting doing nothing else. Don immediately stated that that was impossible; he simply did not have three twenty-minute segments in his day to listen to music. I suggested he schedule the tapes right into his day just as he scheduled patients. When he insisted he was too busy, I countered by questioning the value of being so busy and making so much money when he was so miserable. Don reluctantly agreed to listen to the music.

The next week Don had lost a total of eleven pounds and was jogging each morning and feeling much better. He also reported that he couldn't stand listening to the Golden Voyage music so he hadn't done that. His reason for avoiding the music was that it took too much time and he felt he would be unable to concentrate on the music but would think of many other things. Don was further instructed regarding the importance of taking time for himself and centering himself using the music meditative technique. He was strongly encouraged to force himself to make the time and concentrate as much as he possibly could on seeing the images which were created in his mind by the music. He was taught the eye roll technique and told the benefits of deep relaxation and centering oneself. The great difficulty which Don was having in calming himself was his greatest clue that the meditative centering experience was what he needed more than anything else.

Several weeks later Don reported feeling more relaxed than he had in a long time. I encouraged him to take a weekend vacation alone with his music tapes and the personal tapes I had made for him for deeper relaxation and concentration. He was instructed to avoid people as much as possible and commune only with nature and himself. Don was off for the first weekend alone is his life, along with several deepening tapes. He chose a friend's mountain cabin as his retreat. He took no alcohol or drugs and no paperwork to do or read. His only form of amusement was himself and the beauty of the mountain scenery. Don returned from his weekend reporting that he felt like a new man. He had spent hours meditating and going deeper into himself and had cried over all the pain he had inflicted on himself. The last tape I had prepared for him addressed the issue of complete forgiveness. Don was instructed to look over all the people in his life and to forgive each of them for whatever injustices he had collected. The most difficult and most important forgiveness to be given was to himself. He was instructed to forgive himself for everything in his life for which he had been

101

blaming himself and to replace that blame and anger with love for himself. He was offered the image of seeing himself being filled with the golden light of love. He reported that he spent many hours working at forgiving himself and loving himself and he felt that he had finally made a breakthrough in his depression.

The following months found Don cutting down on his hours at work and spending more time on himself. He joined a group of fellow travelers on the journey into the self using group meditation techniques and reported he was happier than he had ever been. He disposed of his adult toys and realized that money cannot bring happiness. Don now has a smaller, less hectic practice and spends more time with each patient, enjoying helping them to grow and become whole and healthy also. He is much more relaxed with his children and for the first time he can really let go and be a child with them.

Don's success took a lot of hard work. He forced himself to change patterns and do things he would ordinarily avoid. He had spent his whole life avoiding knowing himself. Like so many people, he had always focused on the outside and worked to change things around him. The purpose of the treatment was to get him inside of himself and liking it. What he learned in therapy was that the only real peace and significant change can come from inside oneself. The technique of meditating and centering provided him with the tools for change, but the labor and time and energy had to come from Don. Like so many others, he had finally had enough misery and was willing to pay the price for change.

Category Two—Performance Problems

Performance problems are common in our society. They

come in all sizes, from the subtle anxiety encountered in daily interactions with people to cases of impotence, phobias, and fear of failure or of success. They all have in common the anxiety of performing and being judged. As we grow up we become sensitive to the judgments and reactions of others. We establish our view of ourselves from the views which others have about us. If we are bombarded with negative criticisms from the significant people in our lives, we tend to see ourselves as inadequate. Some people struggle to overcome inadequacy feelings by working hard to achieve high goals, but even when they are successful by the current standards of society, they often hang on to a negative view of themselves. Other people avoid any kind of competition or exposure in an effort to avoid the negative judgments of others. These people frequently underachieve and often isolate themselves in safe little niches where they feel secure. Their basic philosophy is to avoid any kind of performance risk, which might expose them as the inadequate persons they feel they really are.

Whether a person overreacts to a sense of inadequacy by overachieving or isolates himself in underachievement, the result is essentially the same: low self-esteem, loneliness, and sadness. The treatment of performance problems must focus on objective self-appraisal using the highest state of awareness possible. Such anxieties are not cured by your hearing how good you are or how well you did something; until you can see your own real worth, others' praises go over your head. The basic solution is relaxation and centering techniques. From the position of relaxed, aware consciousness you can begin to see yourself more accurately and begin to change your view of yourself from within. All of the external success in the world is not helpful until you can appreciate your own self-worth.

CASE 1—FEAR AND ANXIETY

Mrs. Gold was a 40-year-old Jewish housewife and mother of seven who was experiencing severe debilitating anxiety attacks. She reported she had felt perfectly fine until approximately two years before. At that time she was working in a small store and felt that the walls were closing in on her. She also began having increasing difficulty getting her breath and became anxious and upset over these feelings. The symptoms progressed to such a point that Mrs. Gold was no longer able to drive a car and became frightened to leave her home.

She entered therapy with a psychologist who talked with her about her early life growing up on the East Coast. In addition she was given some breathing exercises and told to drink various kinds of hot teas when she felt the anxiety approaching. During the eighteen months of treatment with the psychologist, Mrs. Gold's symptoms increased to the point where she gave up her job and confined herself to her house except when her husband took her to see the psychologist. She had a severe attack of panic anxiety one afternoon and thought she was dying because of pains in her chest and palpitations of her heart. She was taken to the emergency room, where she was reassured and referred to me. I consulted with the psychologist, who reported that he had done everything he could think of and was happy to transfer the case to someone else.

I began by clarifying with Mrs. Gold how strongly she felt about giving up her symptoms and returning to a normal life. She was adamant that she hated living the way she did and would do anything to change. I prescribed the Golden Voyage tape, Volume I, and demanded that she sit quietly and relax to the music at least ten times a day for the first week. On the second visit Mrs. Gold reported she felt much better and had had no attacks of anxiety during the week. I instructed her in deeper relaxation techniques and made a tape for her, describing the most relaxing scenes from her life. She was also instructed to venture outside the house at least once every day, carrying her tape recorder if she chose.

The following week, Mrs. Gold appeared like a new woman. Her husband reported she had made great progress and was becoming like her old self again. Mrs. Gold reported that she was listening to the tapes up to twenty times a day and had not only gone outside her home but had ventured to the local shopping mall on the bus. She was very proud of her accomplishment, as she had not been on a bus in over five years and had not been to the shopping mall in more than a year. In the final visit Mrs. Gold reported that she had driven herself to the appointment, and although she had had moments of tension, she had overcome them by relaxing herself and bringing the images of calm and peacefulness into her consciousness. She had practiced so much that she could relax herself completely by just taking a few deep breaths. Her husband and family reported a truly dramatic change and all were pleased with her progress.

The essence of Mrs. Gold's successful treatment was her decision and commitment to change herself. She was literally at the end of her rope and couldn't stand another day of the misery in which she was living. I gave her the simple tools of deep relaxation and visualization and she used them to the fullest. She was able to visualize herself leaving the house, and then when she actually left she experienced only minimal anxiety. Mrs. Gold's exceptional motivation to change caused her to practice her relaxation and imagery much more than most people. Her results document her hard work. The problems of acute and chronic anxiety and panic attacks is much more common than many people think. Many suffer needlessly from major and minor fears which could be easily modified and eliminated using the proper techniques.

CASE 2 —IMPOTENCE

Gil was a 30-year-old bachelor who had been engaged to be married three times. Each time he had broken off the relationship shortly before the wedding. He told me he was afraid of getting tied down to one woman and losing his freedom, but it quickly became clear that he was primarily afraid of not being able to perform sexually. Gil had experienced successful intercourse with several casual girlfriends and had been successful with two of his fiancées. However, he had experienced impotence on three occasions and was fearful that he would not be successful in a long-term relationship. His anxiety about his sexual performance caused him to avoid serious dating and he relieved his sexual tension through masturbation.

Gil had been an only child with a powerful and demanding mother and sensitive but ineffective father. He felt that his parents had a relationship of convenience, and he doubted that they had had intercourse in years since there was no evidence of affection between them. His mother continuously nagged Gil about everything he did, and rarely praised him. She always told him how much she loved him, but somehow she didn't behave that way. Gil remembered particularly her disparaging remarks about most of the girls he dated in high school; she never believed any of them were good enough for him. When he graduated from high school, his mother tried to get him to go to a nearby college so he could live at home, but his father encouraged him to get away.

Gil's first sexual experience, which came during his second year of college, was with a cold woman who was very aggressive and practically forced Gil to have intercourse with her. He remembered that initially he had an erection but was unable to sustain it shortly after penetration. Gil later became involved with another woman who was more sensitive to him and he achieved successful intercourse with her. He became engaged to her but broke off shortly before the wedding, feeling marrying her wasn't the right thing to do. His mother did not approve of his choice in any of his three engagements. Gil followed basically the same pattern with his other fiancees, changing his mind before getting married. He viewed himself as not very attractive, not very successful, and not as good as most of the other men he knew. He had incorporated his mother's negative comments into his self-image.

The treatment plan for Gil was to help him get in touch with the good, decent person he really was and erode the negative images of himself from his childhood. I suggested that he avoid situations that might lead to intercourse and instead attend meetings and meet new people at a local self-awareness group. He was given the techniques for relaxation and meditation and encouraged to work at them to get in touch with his deeper inner self. Gil was anxious to be successful and practiced relaxing himself and later developing images of being successful, meeting women, dating, and ultimately having intercourse. In the group he met a number of women who were thoughtful, kind, and loving without making any demands on him. He joined a small meditation group and found the unique experience of being loved unconditionally by the others. He began to feel much stronger and more positive about himself and started dating one of the women in the group. She was a kind, sensitive, loving person who totally accepted Gil and made no demands on him. He developed a strong attachment to her and they agreed to live together. Gil was anxious the first time they slept together but he used the abilities he had learned in relaxation to overcome his anxiety and he was successful. Gil and Suzanne were later married and he has had no further problems with impotence.

The essence of Gil's successful change was his ability to get to a deeper level of himself, beyond the negative programming from his mother. He achieved the state of really knowing himself through the practice of relaxation and meditation, which enabled him to appreciate his uniqueness and goodness. He overcame the negative influences by seeing himself separate from what his mother thought of him. His resultant good feelings about himself, combined with the accepting attitude of Suzanne, completely overcame his performance anxieties about sex.

CASE 3—FEARS OF FAILURE

Mrs. Black was a 52-year-old mother of two grown children, married for thirty years. During the previous five years she had become increasingly dissatisfied with her life and made a decision to return to work as a nursing assistant, which had been her occupation before she had children. Mrs. Black enrolled in a preparatory course to familiarize herself with the new techniques and medicines, and after the initial anxiety of the first class, she did very well, receiving an A in the class. Approximately one month later she and her husband went on an enjoyable vacation, and upon returning home, Mrs. Black applied for work through a nursing registry. She felt quite anxious filling out the application.She was called for work the next day and declined because she felt too anxious and upset to be able to work. She felt her heart racing, sweaty palms, and tension in her neck and head which turned into a headache. Mrs. Black recognized that she needed help and called me.

Mrs. Black reported a long history of nervousness which had become more severe in the previous five years. She had functioned very well as a nursing assistant prior to her marriage and then had been an outstanding wife and mother during the child-rearing years. As her children grew up and began leaving home and needing her less, Mrs. Black found her life more and more empty. She tried an assortment of hobbies but found little satisfaction from them. She recognized that she was becoming increasingly anxious and depressed and had decided that going back to work might be the answer.

When asked why she believed she would fail, she commented that she felt she was just too old to learn the new skills and knowledge required to do a good job. I questioned her for proof to support this belief, particularly in light of her good performance in class. She was unable to prove her incapability to learn new skills and was forced to see her proven ability. Her next belief was that she was just a housewife and was not competent to provide nursing care for ill persons. I again questioned her for evidence to prove her incapability and she could find none. She did report that during the last two years she had taken care of his invalid mother-in-law, and in fact had performed most of the duties required of a nursing assistant. I underscored her proven success. Her last holdout to prove she couldn't do it was that she was too old to compete with the younger people on the jobs. I questioned how her age affected her abilities and once again proved that it was her ideas that were blocking her, not her performance.

I supported Mrs. Black in her proven abilities and helped her to see how she was underrating herself. I pointed out that her fear of failure was preventing her from being successful and feeling good and that there was no legitimate rational basis for her fears. Once she clearly saw that she was capable and in fact had nothing to fear, she was able to accept the job and perform well. She later reported that the first hour on the new job was frightening, but once she got used to the routine she did very well.

These three cases of performance problems demonstrate the relative simplicity with which such problems can be resolved. It is important not to confuse simplicity with being easy, though. The work required to change performance anxieties is substantial but it is not complicated. If you follow the techniques outlined and apply your time and energy to making the change, you will experience significant modifications in your behavior and feelings.

Category Three—Bad Habits

We all know people who have bad habits, and many of us are even willing to admit that there is room for improvement in ourselves. Bad habits are behaviors that are annoying or obnoxious and create a negative interaction with other people. They are never truly useful in achieving success and often lead to failure, especially when the success or failure depends on a positive relationship with others. Most people try to avoid those who have a habit of nagging, impatience, rudeness, short temper, violence, or stubbornness.

Like all other behaviors, these negative habits can be changed if you have enough desire to make the change. Remember, though, that although you can change these characteristics about yourself, it is very unlikely you can change them in another adult. The most significant thing you can do to help others change is to change yourself and become a model for them. A common bad habit, in fact, is nagging others about changing their bad habits. Step back and take a look at yourself and decide what habits of yours need to change. Probably you have had your behavioral patterns for many years and they are considered part of your personality. You do not have to be confined to these behaviors but have the power to change the way you behave.

Most bad habits start out as either things we could get away with or things we needed to do to survive. For instance, the young child who is given heavy responsibility for her younger brothers and sisters often grows up to be a controlling perhaps nagging adult. But the patterns which were necessary to be successful in childhood are no longer effective for an adult. When the adult recognizes that he is behaving in negative, destructive patterns of bad habits, he can consciously go about changing these patterns.

CASE 1—NAGGING

Steve is a 28-year-old highly successful self-employed businessman who felt unsuccessful in establishing meaningful relationships with others. He had been married twice and was considering remarriage, but his fiancée had encouraged him to see me regarding the way he treated people. She loved Steve but found his continual nagging and his disparaging remarks offensive. When she pointed out how he treated her, he could see that he had also treated his first two wives the same way and that he treated his friends and employees in a similar manner.

Steve knew himself to be a perfectionist and demanded a great deal from himself. He demanded the same behavior from those around him, and when they didn't perform as well as he expected, he would belittle them with his criticisms. In essence, no one could do any job as well as Steve. In truth, his fiancée and most of his employees were very talented, creative people who did an excellent job, but Steve would still complain. As a result, Steve had no close friends, nor did he feel he needed any.

Steve was raised by a father who was just like him, and Steve did not like to be around him. He had received constant criticism from his father about everything he did. Steve had vowed never to be like his father, yet here he was repeating the behavior. When Steve recognized that he was behaving very much as his father had treated him, he wanted to change and swore to do anything necessary to break his bad habit. I explained how bad habits become part of us through repetition so that eventually we engage in them automatically. Steve acknowledged that he was unaware of how much he criticized and nagged people but said that since so many people had mentioned it to him, he believed he was doing it.

We began to work on Steve's problem through exercises in increased awareness. Before Steve said something to someone, he was to think about what he was going to say and was to monitor himself regarding whether or not he was nagging. I assured him that this task would be difficult but that he would be surprised to see the results. The following week Steve reported that he had been shocked to realize that he was criticizing people in almost every interaction he had with them. He had been successful in seeing his pattern and had begun to change it by correcting himself before he blurted out the deprecating remarks. Steve continued to work on being aware of himself and in four weeks had made a significant change in his bad habit pattern. He recognized that he was going to have to keep after himself to avoid falling back into the old pattern, but he felt confident he could do so. His fiancée also reported a big change in Steve and both stated they were much happier.

It is not easy to change a long-established habit pattern, but if it is important enough to you you will be successful. Each time you stop yourself and think before you speak or act, you are raising your awareness and getting better control over yourself. Ultimately, the new way of behaving becomes as natural as the old habit and completely replaces it.

CASE 2—SHORT TEMPER

Mrs. Ludwig was a 34-year-old Italian woman, married for thirteen years with a 7-year-old daughter. She came to me because her husband was threatening to leave her if she didn't do something about her violent temper. She explained that she was raised in a family where everyone shouted at everyone else and both her parents had short, violent tempers. It was not at all uncommon for her mother to throw dishes at her father, and she felt that expressing her angry feelings in this way was normal and appropriate. Mrs. Ludwig had married a scientist, who was calm and logical in his reaction to stress. He never lost his temper and raged about as she did, and after thirteen years he described himself as "burnt out" on her temper tantrums. He demanded that she get some help and learn to control herself.

In the first interview, Mrs. Ludwig explained that she did get very angry with her husband frequently and would scream at him and occasionally throw things. She agreed that this was not a successful way of dealing with her husband and desired to be more successful in her marriage as well as in her work. I began by teaching her the deep relaxation technique and encouraging her to listen to the Golden Voyage tapes as often as she could.She was highly motivated and willing to work hard at changing herself.

During the first week, Mrs. Ludwig practiced controlling herself and listened to the tape four or five times a day. When she got into stressful situations, she talked to herself and calmed herself, reminding herself that she could deal rationally and appropriately with the situation. She had no temper tantrums in the first week and felt good about her ability to change. Her husband was skeptical about the permanence of her change, though. I encouraged her to work at being more accepting and loving toward her husband and to stop demanding that he be affectionate, sensitive, and attentive to her. I also suggested that she might try keeping quiet more and not bombard her husband with questions as soon as he walked through the door. She had the habit of putting her husband through an inquisition every time he came home and he resented it. Mrs. Ludwig reluctantly agreed to work at being quieter and letting her husband adjust to being at home before she talked to him.

In the third session Mr. Ludwig was present and reported a dramatic change in his wife. He still wondered, though, if she had really changed or if this was just temporary behavior. I supported Mrs. Ludwig's ability to change herself because she had a very important reason to change. He reported that she had not had any temper outbursts in nearly three weeks and was much more loving and affectionate than he had ever remembered. He stated that he really liked her this way and if she could maintain control over herself he wanted to stay married to her. Mrs. Ludwig also stated that she liked herself better and recalled that this had been the longest period without a temper outburst. On several occasions she had felt angry and wanted to yell at her husband but she had stopped and calmed herself. They both agreed that things were much better between them and they planned to celebrate with a weekend in Palm Springs to get to know each other better.

Mrs. Ludwig cancelled her next appointment, saying that she was "cured." She felt she knew what to do and no longer needed therapy. I agreed that she had done remarkably well and supported her ability to maintain herself without tantrums.

Temper outbursts are not inherited but rather learned behaviors which, through relaxation, can be unlearned and replaced by new ways of behaving. Mrs Ludwig had never truly needed to change until her husband challenged her. She recognized that her bad habits were not useful patterns of behavior and she chose to do what she had to do to change her pattern. Anyone with short temper or violent temper can do the same thing, but it frequently takes some crisis in one's life to motivate him or her to change.

Afterword

This is a practical book which teaches you how to get what you want out of life. The techniques are quite simple but they are not easy. To make significant change in yourself requires energy, commitment, and decision. No big change in your life is going to come about unless you make the effort to do the work required. The habit patterns which you have developed throughout your life are not accidental. You encouraged each of these patterns because it worked at some point in your life. Usually it is not working for you today but is creating problems for you. To make a significant change, you must first look at what the real problem is which you want to change. It is important to focus on what the important issues are and to make a decision to work on only one at a time. The reason for this is to avoid getting into a state of confusion and feeling impotent and helpless. If you focus on one thing at a time, you can ensure success in changing one important aspect of your life. After mastering one significant change in your behavior, you can move on to another and ultimately remake yourself into what you want to be.

The second step in the process is to examine the roadblocks you have thrown up to prevent yourself from being successful. In nearly all cases the reasons you have developed for your being unsuccessful are to be found in the exact words you are using to yourself. For instance, saying to yourself "I just can't lose weight" puts you in a position of total incapability. In this book each of the most commonly held beliefs has been explored so you might gain insight into how these beliefs and the attendant language prevent change. The most common excuses we use are: stages of life, heredity, instincts, emotional illness, medical problems, age, and environment.

116

In the next step, look at how you protect yourself from changing by other strongly held beliefs. Such things as inability, questions, wishes and desires, understanding, self-labeling, predictions, and shoulds have been considered as blocks to changing. In each case of mistaken belief, you were given examples to clarify how these ideas have been maintained and how they stop us from changing.

Perhaps the most overlooked aspect of anyone's life is what they do right. Unfortunately, we live in a world where the primary emphasis is on what we are doing wrong. The truth is that we do much more right than wrong. Each of us has a wealth of experience in being successful but we commonly overlook these successes. This book has explained how you can examine your life and find your successes, and use them to build new patterns of successful behavior. Each of us is in control of what we do. When you begin to understand that all of your behaviors are voluntary, then you are in a better position to change. The book has examined the communications you give to yourself in areas where you are successful and told how they differ from the things you say when you are unsuccessful. In each case there are many examples to prove how each person can achieve success using techniques already present in his or her repertoire.

The questions to ask yourself in preparation for making significant change are detailed in Chapter 5. After answering these questions, you can begin to see that you are capable of making significant change and know what the necessary steps are for making that change. Making a decision to change is not an easy process and requires a real commitment and energy. You worked very hard to get yourself into the mess you are in and you are going to have to work hard to get out of it. When you make a serious decision to change, you will be successful.

In the last section you were taught how to use deep relaxation and self-hypnosis to assist yourself in making the changes you desire. The practice of relaxation and meditation has been proven effective in assisting people since the beginning of time. In addition, visual imagery and visualization assist in making important changes. These techniques, using your right brain, are extremely powerful and quite simple to learn and practice. As with anything else, the more you practice, the better you are. Finally, you have read numerous case histories which detail the use of the techniques in this book. The categories of case histories are Escapes, Performance Problems, and Bad Habits. Each of us will be able to find himself in at least one of these broad categories.

This book has been written to help people overcome their problems and keep from reaching the point where they need professional help. These techniques have been successful in thousands of cases and can work for you. If you work truly hard and still find that you are not successful, then it may be very useful to seek a professional therapist to help you sort out where you are undermining yourself. I believe that you can be just as successful as so many others, if you are really committed to changing yourself.

Good luck!

Index